The Complete Photo Guide To
FRAMING
& DISPLAYING ARTWORK

Creative Publishing
international

First published in the United States of America by
Creative Publishing international, Inc., a member of
Quayside Publishing Group
400 First Avenue North
Suite 300
Minneapolis, MN 55401
1-800-328-3895
www.creativepub.com

ISBN-13: 978-1-58923-422-2
ISBN-10: 1-58923-422-7

10 9 8 7 6 5 4 3 2

Library of Congress Cataloging-in-Publication Data
to come

President/CEO: Ken Fund
VP for Sales & Marketing: Kevin Hamric

Publisher: Winnie Prentiss
Aquisition Editor: Linda Neubauer
Copy Editor: Elizabeth Degenhard
Proofreader: Ellen Goldstein
Creative Director: Michele Lanci-Altomare
Senior Design Managers: Jon Simpson, Brad Springer
Design Manager: James Kegley
Production Managers: Linda Halls, Laura Hokkanen
Book Design & Layout: Tiffany Laschinger
Cover Design: John Barnett, 4eyedesign.com

The Complete Photo Guide To
FRAMING
& DISPLAYING ARTWORK

500 Full-Color How-to Photos

Creative Publishing
international

CONTENTS

INTRODUCTION TO
DO-IT-YOURSELF FRAMING

The Purpose of Picture Framing

Picture framing is a time-honored profession, as well as a popular hobby. Decorating the walls with framed pictures is such an essential part of home décor that rooms usually look bare and "unlived in" without some kind of art hanging in them.

The inspiration for the first frames around pictures (decorative borders painted around wall paintings) was the same as our purpose today: to isolate and enhance images for enjoyable viewing. When art began to be created on portable materials, such as wood panels, canvas, and eventually paper, frames became portable, independent units as well. Over time, various framing practices became established, and picture framing developed into a profession, with specialized tools and materials.

Framed art gives a finished look to room décor. Because framed art can be used in every room, on stairways, and in hallways, a home can use many kinds of framing.

DIY Framing

Years ago, creating professional-looking picture framing at home was a complicated endeavor requiring a carpentry workshop, and good materials were not easy to find. Local craft and hobby stores had little to offer the home framer—just a small selection of premade mats and ordinary frames. Today, the situation is quite different: With the wide variety of tools and materials available at local stores and on the Internet, the do-it-yourself framer can complete fashionable, high-quality picture framing in a fairly small work area without a lot of fancy equipment.

People are attracted to framing for a variety of reasons. Some are artists, needleworkers, or photographers who want to frame their own work. Some are woodworkers interested in exploring a new craft. Many are simply creative people who own artwork that needs to be framed, and are looking for a hands-on way to get the look they really want.

This book is a guide to the entire framing process, from designing the job to hanging the finished piece on the wall. It is not possible to address every framing topic in a single book, because framing is a complex profession, but every attempt has been made to provide the DIY framer with all of the information needed to frame a wide range of art. Methods that use premade materials and "framing from scratch" are both explored. As in any profession that involves methods and techniques, there are disagreements among professional picture framers about the "right way" or "best way" to do things. This book takes a practical approach that explains the current points of view, letting the individual framer make an informed choice.

No prior experience is needed to learn picture framing. The workspace needed is not large, and the necessary equipment ranges from a few hand tools to a complete workshop, depending on the interest of the framer. Some basic skills are required, such as dexterity and a steady hand, but a willingness to learn and practice is probably the most important ability.

Is DIY framing an economical way o frame pictures? It certainly can be. Like any hobby, picture framing may be done with the simplest materials and tools, or with the most elaborate. Usually it is best to start with simple versions to give the craft a try before committing to greater expense—although some people prefer to invest in good equipment right from the start, convinced this is the path to a better finished product with less frustration. Which approach is best depends on personal work style, budget, and the amount of framing anticipated.

Many photographers like to learn DIY picture framing so they can frame their own work.

Parts of a Frame Job

The frame is the outer border and an important decorative element; it also holds the framing package together. Glazing is a sheet of glass or plastic installed in the face of the frame to protect the artwork. A mat surrounds and supports the artwork, and it is an important decorative element; it also keeps the artwork from touching the glazing.

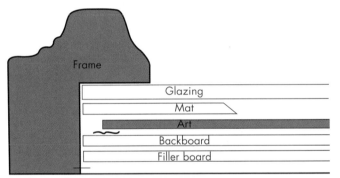

Frame

Glazing

Mat

Art

Backboard

Filler board

Dust cover

The backing board stabilizes the art and supports the art and mats. The filler board fills excess space in the frame and provides additional support.

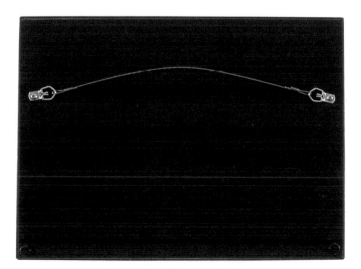

The dust cover protects the contents of the frame and makes an attractive finish. The hanging hardware provides a means for hanging the art on the wall. Bumper pads help keep the frame in place on the wall and protect the wall from scratches made by the frame.

The Goals of Picture Framing

When a DIY framer decides to frame a picture, it may be to fill a space on a wall, create a gift for a friend, or bring out a color to coordinate and complement room décor. Regardless of the reason for doing it, picture framing serves two important purposes for the art and objects it holds: protection and presentation. Framing provides a protective display package while also presenting art in an attractive design of color and style. A framer should consider both goals when choosing materials and methods for framing each piece of art. Which purpose deserves the most priority? The answer may be different for different projects, and the decision usually belongs to the owner of the artwork that will be framed. In most cases, it is possible to achieve the best of both worlds, producing framing that is as protective of the art as possible while also creating a pleasing visual design that suits the environment in which it will be displayed.

To a viewer, picture framing is a presentation of color and design choices; inside the frame, choices of materials and methods play a role in the protection of the art.

Archival, Preservation, or Conservation Framing

The terms "archival," "preservation," and "conservation" are used interchangeably in picture framing to refer to framing that gives artwork the highest level of protection possible. In professional framing, this type of framing is recommended for all valued artwork, whether the value is monetary, historical, or sentimental.

All of the materials used in conservation framing must meet a list of criteria. Many products in the craft industry state on their packages that they are "acid-free." Acid-free is a good thing, because acids are responsible for much of the deterioration of artwork. But acids are not the only source of harm, so products used in conservation framing need to have other qualities as well. They must be nonstaining, and they must not deteriorate over time, exposing the art to debris or harmful gases. To be truly archival, framing must also be "reversible," so that the art

Many products sold for scrapbooking and other paper crafts are acid-free and meet other criteria for conservation framing. Read the packages to determine the suitability.

This original pastel drawing is framed using archival methods and materials, which will give it the most protective environment that framing can provide.

Museum curators and professional framers must adhere to strict standards of conservation framing, because they are responsible for protecting the present and future health of the art and objects they handle. They are trusted custodians (not owners) of the work they frame. DIY framers are in a different position: All decisions about framing art and objects are completely within their authority, and they may set standards as they please. (Although when framing highly valued items belonging to friends and family, it is prudent to consider conservation framing materials.) So how should a beginner make choices?

The best approach for the DIY framer is to learn about the materials and methods of conservation framing, and then make educated decisions on a project-by-project basis. The difference between regular framing and conservation framing is a matter of a few simple choices. Throughout this book, conservation framing materials and methods are discussed when applicable. The materials are readily available. The cost is a bit higher but well worth the expense to protect valued art. Even when framing decorative artwork that is not meant to last for generations, there are often practical choices that are easy to make. For example, ordinary clear adhesive tape yellows, stains what it touches, and eventually dries so much that it releases its hold, while opaque Magic Mending Tape has a clean, long-lasting adhesive that remains stable for decades. So why not use the stable one instead?

can be removed from the frame in the future with no harm caused by the framing. This is the standard used by museums and by most professional picture framers. This means, for example, that a particular type of adhesive tape may be acid-free, nonstaining, and nondeteriorating, but the adhesive may be so strong that it cannot be removed from the art without the use of chemical solvents; some of that solvent will inevitably soak into the artwork, which constitutes a permanent alteration that could discolor or otherwise damage the art in the future. This tape would be unsuitable for strict conservation framing. Many of the products discussed in this book are described as "non-archival" not because they are harmful to the art, but because they alter the art in some permanent way.

How Long Will It Last? Enemies of Framed Art

Many factors influence the life of a framed picture. For most artwork, longevity comes from a combination of proper framing and protection from environmental damage while the framing is on display.

Cause of Harm	Source of Harm	Potential Damage	Protection Framing Can Provide
Handling	Hands, poor storage, faulty repairs	Fingerprints, creases, stains	Complete protection if art is covered with glazing
Insects	Tasty items in frame, such as wool or paste	Holes, overall deterioration	Good protection, unless insects are sealed inside the frame
Moisture/ Humidity	Damp or steamy places, such as bathrooms, kitchens, screened porches, boats, shore cottages	Warping, buckling, and mold	Framing slows absorption a bit, but this problem must be controlled by placement of framed art or by controlling the environment
Air Pollution	Chemicals, insecticides, cooking grease, fireplace smoke and ash	Stains and discoloration	Framing provides good protection if art is covered with glass or acrylic
Light	Sunshine, incandescent, fluorescent, halogen, picture lights	Fading	Proper framing can help, but fading is best controlled by avoiding strong light
Heat and Cold	Extreme temperatures and extreme changes	Warping, buckling	Can be controlled by proper framing and choice of hanging location
Acids and Gases	Framing materials or the art itself	Discoloration and deterioration	Proper framing can prevent damage caused by materials and mitigate internal weaknesses

A Word about Professional Picture Framers

When should a DIY framer consult a professional? Whenever a project is too complex or too large for the equipment, skill level, or workspace available; when special materials not available to the DIY framer are needed; or when the artwork in question is so fragile or valuable that professional help is warranted.

If you choose to have your artwork framed by a professional custom picture framer, this book can help you be an informed customer. Knowledge of color choices, design, and framing standards will help you to make decisions at the frame shop and evaluate the custom work you have done.

Most professional picture framers enjoy their profession and work hard to be very good at it. However, the expertise and experience of professional picture framers varies. To choose a framer, look for indications of professional standards.

In the U.S. and Canada, membership in the Professional Picture Framers Association (PPFA) lets customers know that a framer is interested in staying active within the industry and keeping up with current standards. The Fine Art Trade Guild (FATG) is the trade association in the UK. Both organizations offer certification programs. Some chain stores have their own training programs and successful candidates earn in-house certification. There are also picture framing schools that offer training. Look for certificates or signage that indicates the framer has taken classes or participated in training. Or just talk to the framer about how they got into the profession—some very fine framers learned the job simply by working for years in good frame shops.

Word-of-mouth can be a good way to find a professional framer. If a friend, neighbor, or family member recommends a business, it means they are satisfied enough to be proud of their choice.

PICTURE FRAMES

The Purpose of the Frame

A picture frame has two important functions: It is the outermost border of the visual presentation of the art, and it holds all of the materials together in a secure package. The typical frame is four straight lengths of picture frame moulding (the professional term for sticks of frame material), cut with a 45-degree angle at each end, and joined together into a rectangle.

The variety of ready-made picture frames available today makes it easy for the Do-It-Yourself framer to create any style of framing, from traditional to trendy.

Anatomy of a Picture Frame

Physical structure is an important part of the right frame for each project, but it is the vast variety of available styles that makes the visual aspect of choosing frames so interesting and fun. A frame may be rustic, formal, ornate, playful, or contemporary. The finish might be rough, smooth, gilded, or shiny. By combining and redesigning elements from centuries of history, and employing new finishing techniques, the variety of designs, colors, and finishes available in picture frames today covers a range from faithful historical reproductions to completely new creations.

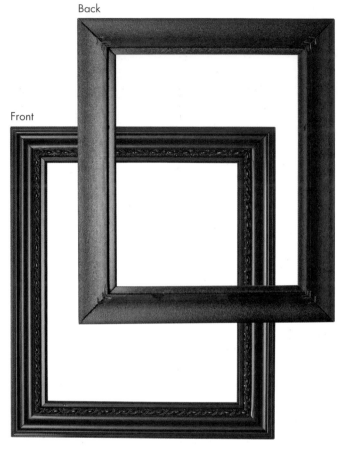

Back

Front

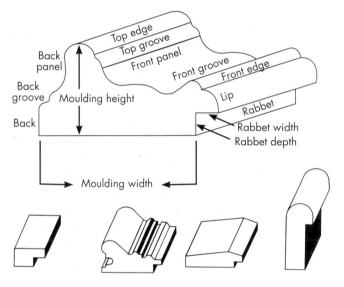

A profile view looks at a moulding from the side to reveal its basic shape. These are a few of the common moulding profiles in today's picture framing market.

Moulding is the professional term for sticks of wood, metal, or other material that have a ledge in the back to hold framing materials and a face that is designed for decorative presentation.

Historic Styles of Frames

Over the centuries, different frame styles developed to suit the current fashion in art and furniture—especially furniture. Historically accurate reproductions are available, particularly to meet the needs of collectors and museums, but many of the frames available today are adaptations of classic styles, representing a combination of different historical elements on one frame.

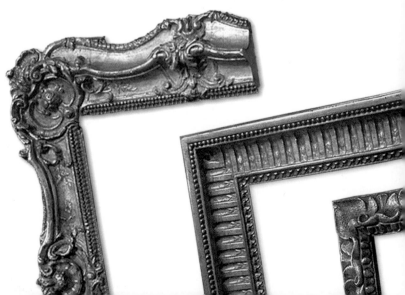

Measuring Frames

There are three sizes that can be discussed when measuring frames. There is the outside size, which is the outer dimension of the frame. There is the visual opening size, which is the opening of the frame when measured from its face. Finally, there is the rabbet size, which is the interior size of the frame when measured from the back, from one side wall of the frame to the opposite side wall. This interior area, including the side wall and the small ledge designed to hold the glass and other materials in the frame, is called the "rabbet." Both the rabbet width and the rabbet depth can be important when framing art and objects.

Materials that are installed in picture frames (such as wood, paper, and fabric) expand and contract with changes in heat and humidity. To accommodate these changes without causing wrinkled artwork or broken glass, picture frames are made with an "allowance." The allowance is usually ⅛" (3 mm) (but sometimes less or more), providing comfortable space for the framing materials. This means that a so-called 8" × 10" (20.3 × 25.4 cm) frame, when measured tightly across the interior, is usually 8⅛" × 10⅛" (20.6 × 25.7 cm); it is made to hold artwork and glass that measure 8" × 10" (20.3 × 25.4 cm). Occasionally there is a skimpy allowance, or even no allowance, so every frame must be measured before the materials it will hold can be prepared.

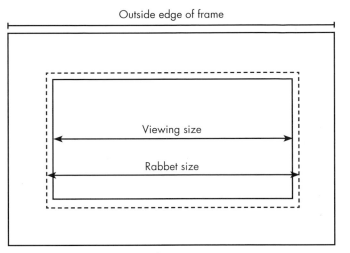

Outside edge of frame

Viewing size

Rabbet size

Viewing size is the area seen from the front. Rabbet size is the measurement of the materials inside the frame. Typically ¼" under the viewing edge. Outside size is the area of the entire frame

Ready-Made Frames

Ready-made frames are just what they claim to be—pre-built picture frames ready to house artwork, mats, glass, and other framing materials. These frames have been readily available for decades in a limited range of styles and sizes, but in recent years the availability of ready-made frames has greatly expanded. The selection now available in hobby, craft, and home improvement stores, in catalogs, and online is extensive and includes a fine variety of styles and colors.

Ready-made frames are typically manufactured from wood, metal, composite resin, or plastic. The quality ranges from very cheap to almost professional, and everything in between.

It is sometimes possible to find raw wood ready-made frames to finish yourself with stain or paint. These are great for times when matching a color or furniture finish is really important, or for experimenting with faux finishes, such as marbling.

Some do-it-yourself framers think using ready-made frames spoils the fun: They enjoy the carpentry skills and equipment needed to cut and build quality frames, and they consider this an important part of framing. But for many of today's home framers, the ability to produce very attractive framed pictures using ready-made frames, without the need for a saw or workshop, is an essential part of the appeal!

Ready-made frames come in so many sizes, finishes, and styles, it is possible to create an endless variety of DIY framing using only these frames.

Quick Frames

These frames are ready-to-go units. They don't require any tasks that could really be called picture framing. Just open them up, pop the flat artwork inside (there isn't usually room for anything thick), and close them. They are almost always made in standard sizes.

Photo frames are made for common photo sizes such as 5" × 7" (12.7 × 17.8 cm) and 8" × 10" (20.3 × 25.4 cm). They come in a huge variety of styles and colors, including ornate traditional, sleek modern, playful, even whimsical. They may be made of wood, metal, molded resin, plaster, plastic, glass, and other materials. Photo frames come with glass or plastic to protect the face of the art, and usually have an "easel back" with an extendable leg that allows the frame to stand on a table or other surface; depending on their construction, they may or may not be able to hang on a wall.

Plastic box frames have a cardboard insert that fits snugly into a five-sided clear plastic face; they hang from a nail in a wall. Clip frames hold the art between a sheet of glass or plastic and a firm backing board, all included in the package; they are made to hang. There are also complete framing packages available in a variety of sizes, even poster size, that include frame, mat, and glass—very fast and convenient.

Although these quick frames won't expand or exercise your picture framing skills, they have useful purposes and can be an important part of the design plan for room décor. An assortment of coordinated photo frames can be grouped on a tabletop or scattered throughout a large bookcase. Six plastic box frames lining a hallway or hung close together in a block arrangement make a simple, contemporary display that is great for areas where glass breakage might be a problem.

Plastic box frame.

This typical photo frame has a backing board that slides into a slot in the frame, equipped with an easel back for standing and hooks for hanging on a wall.

Standard Sizes in Picture Framing

Ready-made frames are generally available in a range of standard sizes, based primarily on standard photo sizes. The most popular sizes are 5" × 7" (12.7 × 17.8 cm), 8" × 10" (20.3 × 25.4 cm), 11" × 14" (27.9 × 35.6 cm), and 16" × 20" (40.6 × 50.8 cm). As discussed earlier, the size stated on the frame refers to the size of glass and other materials it will hold; the rabbet size of the frame itself will be slightly larger, approximately $1/8$" (3 mm) bigger in both length and width.

Standard Sizes

4×5	8×10	12×16	20×24	26×32	40×48
4×6	8½×11	14×18	22×28	30×40	40×60
5×7	9×12	16×20	24×30	32×40	48×96
6×8	11×14	18×24	24×36	36×48	

Beyond the Rectangle

Ready-made frames come in other shapes besides the typical rectangle, including oval, circle, and octagon. Availability is limited to a few sizes and styles. Ovals are the most common shape, usually in standard sizes between 5" × 7" (12.7 × 17.8 cm) and 16" × 20" (40.6 × 50.8 cm). Even less common is the spandrel style: a circle or oval opening in a rectangular frame. A small assortment of special-purpose frames are also available, such as triangular frames for folded military flags, or square frames for scrapbook pages.

Sectional Wood and Metal Frames

In addition to pre-built frames, there are sectional frames, which are wood or metal (normally aluminum) mouldings cut with a traditional 45-degree corner miter. In craft and hobby stores, they are sold in pairs, along with the hardware for assembly; two packages, or two pairs of moulding, make one frame. The wood finishes are typically oak, cherry, black, or white, and occasionally raw unfinished. The metal finishes are typically shiny silver, gold, and sometimes black or frosted silver or gold.

In stores, the sections are sold in the most popular standard sizes, so buyers can make traditional-size frames; but because sectional frames are purchased in pairs, it is possible to make many nontraditional combinations. Instead of an 11" × 14" (27.9 × 35.6 cm) frame, one can make an 11" × 24" (27.9 × 61 cm) frame or a 14" (35.6 cm) square.

Mail-order and Internet sources offer a wider selection of styles and colors (including a deep profile made to accommodate art on canvas or to use as a shadow box for objects up to about ¾" [1.9 cm] thick), which can be ordered cut to the size needed.

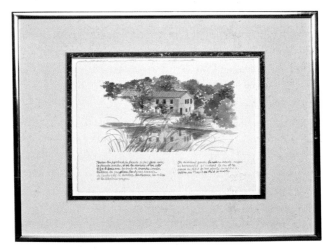

Metal sectional frames provide a sleek, contemporary finish.

These are the most common profiles of metal sectional frames.

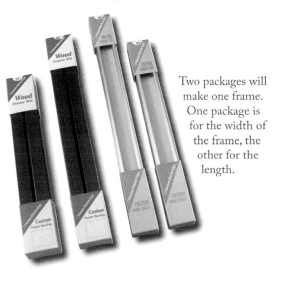

Two packages will make one frame. One package is for the width of the frame, the other for the length.

Custom Sizes for the DIY Framer

Lots of great framing can be done using standard-size wood frames; for most artwork, there is a way to create an attractive presentation that conforms to those sizes. But what about artwork that just doesn't seem to fit? What if you need an unusual size? A long, narrow frame? A big square? Sectional frames offer some flexibility, but there is a limited selection of color and style. Fortunately, mail-order catalogs and Internet suppliers offer an extensive variety of custom-made frames, so a DIY framer can get just the size that is needed. These may be called "pre-built," "custom-made," "completed frames," or several other names. On the local scene, frame shops may be willing to sell empty custom frames. If the frame supplier does not specify its allowance policy ($\frac{1}{8}$" [3 mm] is customary, but $\frac{1}{16}$" [2 mm] is sometimes used), ask to be sure that one is included.

Recycled Frames

Antique stores, garage sales, and flea markets can be a great source for picture frames; you never know what you'll find. Old frames can be re-glued and re-nailed at the corners. They can be refinished or repainted. But they must be stable and sturdy—watch out for dry, brittle, or rotten or badly warped wood. The sizes vary because many are homemade or custom made. Antique picture frame glass usually has visible bubbles and ripples. Whether this is charming or ugly is a matter of opinion; it is highly valued by collectors of vintage art, who enjoy the authentic presentation this brings to the framing. One type of old ready-made frame has convex glass, which rises in a rounded curve that may be several inches (centimeters) high at the center. Old frames can often be cleaned using household furniture cleaning products. Use a soft cloth and a soft brush to get into nooks and crannies.

Old frames can be fun to use in DIY framing, but watch out for brittle or warped wood, which may make the frame unusable.

Inside Frames

In addition to the many kinds of frames that serve as the outer border of the framing, there are some frame mouldings made to accessorize frames and mats. The two most common types are liner moulding and fillet moulding.

Liners are flat or sloped moulding, usually covered with fabric, such as linen, which serve as mats for art on canvas, and are also used in shadow boxes. Fillets are narrow strips of moulding that come in many styles, which are used to provide a dimensional accent line in a frame or a mat. Liners and fillets may come already attached to a ready-made frame, or they can be ordered in custom sizes to be attached by the framer.

Special Types of Frames

Some frame styles are designed to work with particular types of art. For example, a frame for stained glass has a slot made to hold a piece of leaded glass. A floater frame has a recessed interior made especially for displaying art on canvas. If ordering a specialty frame by mail order or online, check with the supplier to find out how this type of frame should be measured.

The narrow beaded strip surrounding the mat opening is a fillet. Fillet moulding comes in many styles; this one was chosen because it matches the beading on the frame.

A shadow box frame is made to hold objects; it has extra depth to accommodate the thickness of the items. This ready-made frame has a slot for glass near the front of the frame.

The flat white border with a gold lip is a linen-covered liner. The liner moulding fits inside the frame, and the art rests in the rabbet of the liner.

MATS AND MATBOARDS

The Purpose of the Mat

Matting is a border that surrounds and supports artwork. It is sometimes called a "window mat" because the border is created by cutting an opening in a piece of board. This opening may be a circle, oval, octagon, or other shape, but most often it is a rectangle. A mat may be made from various materials, but it is usually made from matboard (page 24). Mats may be used on all types of paper artwork, on needlework, and in some shadow boxes.

The mat plays two very important roles in framing: protection and presentation. The window mat and backing board (a solid sheet of board the same size as the outer dimensions of the mat) form a sandwich that encloses the art, creating essential air space and protecting the art from contact with the glass and any other materials in the frame. This important protection happens invisibly within the frame, but the other function of the mat, presenting the artwork, is all show.

The decorative aspect of matting is crucial to successful framing. Along with the frame, the color, texture, and dimensions of the mat determine how a piece of framed art is perceived. It is literally the window through which the art is viewed. The colors chosen for a mat can feature a color in the artwork, coordinate artwork to suit room décor, or just tickle the framer's fancy. The size and shape of the mat can also be used to accommodate different design goals.

The mat creates a window that enhances the visual presentation of framed art while also providing a protective environment.

What is a Matboard?

When picture framers use the word "board," they are usually referring to various types of paper board sheets. Matboard is a type of paper board made specifically for picture framing. There are two main types of construction. The most common by far is made of layers of paper, with a color sheet attached to the top and a liner sheet on the bottom. This type of matboard comes in hundreds of surface paper colors and many patterns, such as marbled, speckled, or printed with designs. The core of the board, which shows when the mat is cut with a traditional bevel, is usually some version of white or off-white, although there are some specialty matboards with a black or other color core. A second and much less common kind of matboard is made by compressing cotton pulp into a solid sheet, with color throughout the board. This method is used to make fine-quality boards for museums, art collectors, and professional framers to store and frame highly valued artwork. This board may sometimes be called "rag" board; the term comes from the history of paper manufacturing that included the use of cotton rags.

The thickness of a matboard varies by type of board and manufacturer, but it is generally in the $\frac{1}{16}$" (2 mm) range. This thickness provides a sturdy support for artwork, and the core creates an attractive bevel that slants toward the artwork when the opening is cut with a 45-degree mat cutter. Thicker boards (called 8-ply) are also available for a deeper bevel. Matboard is made in two standard sizes: 32" × 40" (81.3 cm × 1 m) and 40" × 60" (1 × 1.5 m), although some framing supply distributors sometimes make smaller pieces available.

Matboards are available in a range of colors to suit the wide variety of artwork they must accommodate.

Acids in Matboards

The term "acid-free" is seen widely in the craft, hobby, and picture framing industries, as people become more aware of the harm that acids can cause. Matting is one place in picture framing where acidity really matters, because the matting will be in continuous direct contact with the artwork, and acids are harmful to most types of art. Acids can cause artwork to become yellow and brittle. Over time, acids in matboards can create a golden brown "burn mark" wherever the acidic mat touches the art. Because there is sometimes "acid migration," meaning acids can move around in the frame, even acidic boards that do not touch the art can cause harm.

There are two ways for a product to be acid-free. First, it may be inherently non-acidic, as is the case with cotton, polyester, and acrylic. The second way to be acid-free is by "neutralizing" the acids in a product. With paper products, such as matboards, the neutralizing is accomplished by adding a highly alkaline substance such as calcium carbonate (the essential ingredient in baking soda) to the manufacturing process. It is common practice to add not just enough calcium carbonate to make the paper products neutral pH, but also a little extra to create a buffer. These "buffered" products will remain acid-free even when new acids are encountered—for a while. How long will it be before deteriorating wood fibers and acids from air pollution use up all of the buffering, and the product becomes acidic? This question is a source of debate in the paper industry, but for matboards, it is probably years and might even be decades.

About "Lignin-Free"

Some craft products state that they are lignin-free. Lignin is a highly acidic substance found in plants, including wood, and is responsible for deterioration in paper and boards, such as in the yellowing of newsprint. Because products can be made acid-free by neutralizing rather than removing the acids present in the product, there may be lignin still present in an acid-free product; this lignin could become harmful to framed artwork in the future if the neutralizer wears off. All lignin is removed from or neutralized in archival paper and boards such as conservation and museum matboards.

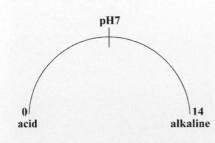

Products measuring higher than 7 on the pH scale are alkaline, while products measuring below 7 are acidic. Products that measure exactly 7 are considered neutral, or acid-free.

This vintage print shows an acid burn where the acidic mat damaged the paper.

Types of Matboard

There are several types of matboard. Different types serve different purposes. The ones listed opposite are the most common, but as companies design unique products to compete with one another, variations are created. By reading the basic information about the three basic types, it should be possible to evaluate the suitability of any type of matboard.

Standard Matboard

This "regular" matboard is made with an acidic wood pulp core (usually buffered), with wood pulp or cotton surface papers (typically not buffered.) The core is usually off-white or cream, and may darken with age as acids in the board act on the wood pulp fibers. Some boards may have a white or black core. If buffered, standard matboards may last for decades without significant change, so it is suitable for framing all types of decorative art. Standard matboard is available in a wide range of surface paper colors. This is the most readily available and most popular board for the do-it-yourself picture framer.

Museum Matboard

This board is a solid sheet made from compressed 100% cotton pulp. Although cotton is naturally acid-free, these boards are usually buffered to create a slightly alkaline chemistry. It is also available unbuffered for certain types of old photographs that are sensitive to alkalinity. Because the board is a solid sheet, the surface, core, and back are all the same color. The color range is limited, mostly white, cream, and neutral colors plus a small selection of pastel colors and black. It is used in museums and in professional framing for highly valued art.

Conservation Matboard

This board is made with a purified wood pulp (conservation board) or natural cotton (rag) core and surface papers. All acids, lignin, and other harmful ingredients are removed, then all parts of the board are buffered to protect against environmental acids. This is the board recommended by many professional framers for most artwork, because it offers excellent protection for the art and can be trusted to remain stable for many years. The core of these boards is usually white, and will stay white. A few colors are available with a black core. Conservation and rag matboard is available in a wide range of surface paper colors. Retailers may call this "archival," "conservation," or "museum grade" matboard.

Unsuitable Boards for Mats

Mats can be cut from poster board, corrugated cardboard, even construction paper. But these products are not suitable for quality picture framing. They are made for temporary display purposes, and they will fade and deteriorate over time. They are also highly acidic, damaging artwork if left in contact with it for a long period.

The Size of the Mat

How big should a mat border be? To do its job protecting the artwork, the mat can have fairly narrow borders. But to do its other job—creating an attractive presentation for the art—it usually needs more.

Beginners usually like small mat borders, even on large pictures. They fear that too much matting will distract from the art. In fact, narrow mat borders can be very distracting, creating too many lines surrounding the art in a target effect. The lines become the key attraction rather than the art. Wider mats provide a visual breathing space between the art and the frame that is more comfortable for most viewers.

Proportion also matters, of course. In general, the width of the mat borders should increase as the size of the artwork increases: a 1½" (3.8 cm) mat border may appear adequate on an 8" × 10" (20.3 × 25.4 cm) photo but would look skimpy to most viewers if used on a 16" × 20" (40.6 × 50.8 cm) photo.

In recent years, the popularity of wide mat borders has grown into an established style. Once used mainly by museums, then adopted by collectors of fine art for displaying valued pieces—especially contemporary art—wide mat borders are now popular for all types of matted art. The width depends on the size of the art, but the look is expansive, with a broad band of matting between the art and the frame.

The choice of the "right" mat borders is a matter of personal perception. As discussed in the section about

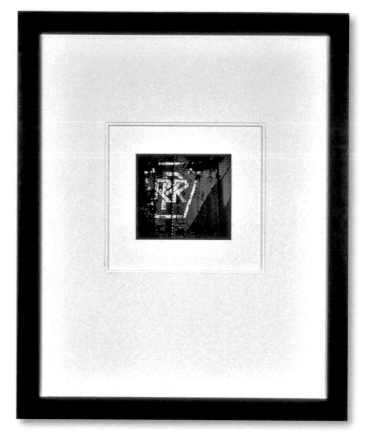

color (page 54), a person's preferences are individual and are formed over time by many influences. They may change as a person matures, learns more, or becomes attracted to new trends. To decide what you like best, look at framed art in magazines, television shows, furniture stores, department stores, homes, offices, museums—anywhere framed art is displayed.

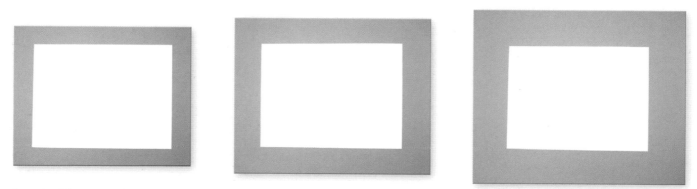

In each of these examples, one mat opening size is shown with different sizes and proportions of borders. Deciding which looks best is a matter of personal perception.

MATS AND MATBOARDS   29

Mat Styles and Their Visual Effects

A variety of mat styles have developed over time, to suit different styles of art and décor, and different visual preferences. They create a mood or character for the art they display.

Single Mat with Equal Borders

This is the most basic standard mat. All four borders surrounding the window opening are the same width. This provides a simple, straightforward presentation for any type of art, with the color and texture of the matboard surface providing the character.

Multiple Opening Mat

Separate openings are cut in one mat to display a number of items in individual windows. The openings may be one size and shape, or a variety of different sizes and shapes. This type of mat is usually used with photographs, trading cards, stamps, or other collectibles. Proportion and balance are important considerations when designing the layout of a multiple opening mat.

Double Mat

The double mat is literally two mats on top of each other. A small amount of the bottom mat is revealed in the opening of the top mat. The exposed lip is typically between ⅛" (3 mm) and ½" (1.3 cm) wide. The inner mat may be the same color as the top mat but most often it is a different color. A double mat not only creates physical and visual depth suitable for any style or size of art, but is considered a finished, professional-looking choice. Triple mats, are also occasionally used.

Weighted Bottom

A weighted bottom mat usually has a slightly extended lower border, although it may sometimes be more distinctly elongated. Some say this suits a natural human preference for a solid base. It may also derive from the Golden Mean theory of balance and measurement studied by artists and architects. Whatever the reason, this style is very popular for many types of art.

Museum Mat

A museum mat has significant mat borders at the top and sides, and a distinctly extended lower border. The name comes from the use of this style by art museums for displaying drawings, engravings, and watercolor paintings. Museums prefer to use white, off-white, gray, or other neutral colors, but some people prefer more intensity. In home décor, the museum mat is used to convey a sense of importance, elegance, or contemporary style.

Oriental Mat

Narrow on two opposite sides, much wider on the remaining two sides, this style is meant to mimic the proportions of art on scrolls. The narrow borders are typically about one-third to one-fourth the width of the wide borders. This style is used most often with Asian art prints or paintings on silk, but it works well on any elongated artwork.

Arched Mat

The curved arch has a classical, traditional, or romantic character. The feeling of antiquity makes it appropriate for Renaissance or classical art or vintage photographs. The feeling of romance makes it suitable for wedding and anniversary photos.

Print Mat

This style has wide sides, with narrower top and bottom borders. This relative newcomer was born out of a rule that says the paper surrounding original artwork should not be trimmed, coupled with the habit of publishers printing original limited edition prints on oversized sheets of paper. This usually results in a very large mat that has a contemporary character.

Oval Mat

An oval opening has a romantic or old-fashioned character. Because the corners of the art will be hidden, oval openings work best when the image is centered. It is often used on vintage photos, wedding photos, old-fashioned silhouette portraits, and needlework. A special mat cutter is required to cut an oval.

Fabric-covered Mat

The texture of fabric adds depth and dimension to the framing design. Some matboards are available with fabric already attached, but custom versions can be made. Linen, silk, suede, and velvet are among the most popular fabric choices, although any medium-weight, even-weave fabric is suitable. It is typically used to add rich character to framing, but it can also be rustic or playful, depending on the fabric chosen.

French Mat

This refers to a style of mat surface decoration that originated in Europe for framing watercolors and engravings, but it is also attractive on documents, photographs, and art prints. The French mat consists of ink lines surrounding the mat opening and panels of watercolor washes between the lines. There may be just two lines and one wash of color, or a series of lines and panels. Depending on the colors and design, French mats can look elegant, pretty, or important.

Embellished Mat

Stickers and other paper decorations can be applied to the surface of a mat. A single monogram in one corner, or perhaps a small decorative design in all four corners, can feel formal or elegant. Numerous colorful embellishments scattered all over the mat can look exuberant or playful.

Using Ready-made Mats

The mats sold in craft, hobby, art supply, and other stores may be called ready-made, precut, or premade mats. When shopping for a ready-made mat, consider both the outside size, which is the frame size, and the window size, which is the opening for the artwork. The dimensions for both the outside and window size are based on traditional photograph sizes. The most common outside sizes, which can be found almost everywhere that sells ready-made mats, are 5" × 7" (12.7 × 17.8 cm), 8" × 10" (20.3 × 25.4 cm), 11" × 14" (27.9 × 35.6 cm), and 16" × 20" (40.6 × 50.8 cm). Take a look at the chart at right for a more complete list of typical mat sizes and the openings they are likely to have. Larger and more diverse sizes may be available in stores that have an extensive framing supply department. For example, to suit the current popularity of wide mat borders, some stores sell a 16" × 20" mat with an 8" × 10" opening. These may be called "gallery mats" or "museum mats" by manufacturers, and some are made using premium-quality 8-ply museum board.

Most ready-made mats are single mats or double mats with the same size border on all four sides. When the borders cannot be equal (because, for example, an 8" × 10" [20.3 × 25.4 cm] opening cannot fit with equal borders into an 11" × 14" [27.9 × 35.6 cm] mat), the excess matting is usually divided equally between the two opposite borders. The mat border on a ready-made mat is usually adequate rather than ample, but there are some exceptions.

Ready-made mats are available in a variety of colors, usually in standard sizes.

Rough Edges

The openings of some ready-made mats are stamped out; others are cut by dull blades. Either way, the result can be loose bits of paper or board on the interior edges of the opening. Trim and smooth rough spots and stray bits with a sharp craft knife and an emery board.

Ready-made Mat Sizes

Outer Mat Size	Typical Window Opening Size
5" X 7"	3" X 5"
8" X 10"	5" X 7"
8½" X 11"	5" X 7"
9" X 12"	5" X 7"
11" X 14"	8" X 10"
12" X 16"	8" X 10"
14" X 18"	11" X 14"
16" X 20"	11" X 14"
20" X 24"	16" X 20"

Ready-made mats are available in basic colors, such as white, black, and cream; a few classic colors such as navy, maroon, baby pink, and baby blue; and a handful of "fashion colors" that are changed over the years as different décor colors go in and out of style.

Ready-made mats are easy to use. They almost always come with a backing board. The quality varies, so a particular mat may or may not be suitable, depending on the framing project. Most ready-made mats found today are at least decent quality, typically buffered wood pulp boards, but read the label and look for the term "acid-free" to be sure. Fine-quality conservation and museum board ready-made mats are available in some stores and from online sources.

GLAZING: GLASS AND ACRYLIC

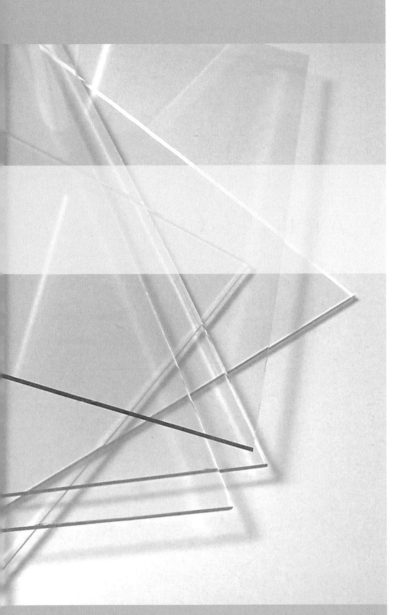

The Purpose of Glazing

The transparent sheet of glass or plastic (acrylic) that is placed in the face of a picture frame is called glazing. Glazing provides a protective cover for the artwork in a frame, shielding the art from airborne dust, grease, household cleaning chemicals—and fingerprints. A few kinds of art can be framed without glazing (such as oil paintings on canvas and some types of needlework), but most framed artwork benefits from the protection of glass or plastic.

There are different types of picture framing glazing to suit different projects, available in glass or acrylic. Local glass and plastic suppliers may carry what you need. Many online sources sell only acrylic, due to shipping concerns about breakage, although some sell glass in the smaller standard sizes.

Glass provides protection from dust, fingerprints, and airborn particles such as cleaning sprays, and helps to keep environmental humidity from affecting the contents of the frame.

Glass for Picture Framing

The typical glass for picture framing is high-quality, single-strength float glass, which is about $\frac{1}{10}$" (2.5 mm) thick and has very few flaws. Local companies may sell this as window glass, but be sure to get single strength—double strength is too heavy for most framing purposes and is so thick that its green tint can alter the colors of the art and matting. Ask about the quality: Some window glass has bubbles and other marks that may show in the framing. Glass for picture frames is sold in a few standard sizes at craft and hobby stores, and in single sheets or cartons of multiple sheets from a few online sources.

Plastic for Picture Framing

The plastic used in professional picture framing is acrylic, and it is the best plastic for do-it-yourself framers as well. It will not yellow for many years, and it is chemically inert, safe for use on valuable art. Acrylic is less than half the weight of glass, and it does not shatter into razor-sharp pieces if broken. This makes it great for framing that will be shipped, framing for kids' rooms, and framing for any vulnerable area, where it might be knocked from the wall. The thickness used by framers ranges from about $\frac{1}{8}$" (3 mm) thick for most frames to $\frac{1}{4}$" (6 mm) thick for very large frames (larger than 24" × 36" [61 × 91.4 cm]).

Acrylic can be purchased in large sheets or cut to size at some local glass supply companies, in a few standard sizes at craft and hobby stores, and in single sheets or cartons of multiple sheets from online sources. Because the surface of acrylic is easily scratched, a special paper is applied to both sides during manufacturing. This should be left in place until ready to finish the framing. When the paper is removed, lots of static is created, which will attract dust and other tiny debris.

Avoid styrene or any thin plastic, even though it may be advertised for picture framing: This low-quality glazing quickly yellows and warps.

Why Glazing Should "Keep Its Distance"

Although glazing is generally a good protection for artwork, it should not be pressed against the surface of the art. During changes in temperature or humidity, moisture can condense on the glazing, causing mold or mildew to form, and making the art stick to the glazing (especially glossy, art-like photographs). Damage from environmental changes is much more of a problem with glass than plastic, because glass is a much stronger heat conductor.

The solution to this problem is space between the art and glazing, and there are several ways to create it. Matting is the simplest and most common method. For frame jobs in which no matting is used, special products are made to hold the glass in place while keeping the artwork away from it.

EconoSpace is made especially for creating spance between the artwork and glazing in a frame. EconoSpace consists of a hollow rectangle that holds the glazing close to the front of the frame, and separates the glazing from the art. Made of pH–neutral plastic, EconoSpace is suitable for conversion framing.

Types of Glazing for Picture Framing

Both glass and acrylic are available in the following styles:

Clear. This is regular glass or acrylic. The type suitable for framing is crystal clear and virtually free from bubbles and other flaws. It gives a sharp view of framed art, but its shiny surface causes glare that can be distracting.

Non-Glare, Non-Reflective, or Anti-Reflective. One or both sides of this glazing are etched to minimize glare, resulting in a soft, frosted finish. Visibility is clear and sharp when the glazing is near the art, but it becomes hazy when used with deep mats or in shadow boxes.

UV-Filtering. Light is necessary to enjoy framed art, but light is a source of damage to art, especially ultraviolet light. UV-filtering glazing shields the art from 95% to 99% of ultraviolet light in the range considered most harmful. This does not mean the frame can be hung in bright sunlight with no fading, but it does provide a measure of protection for art hung in normal lighting situations.

Museum. This glazing is used by museums and professional framers to give valued artwork the maximum light protection and an outstanding view at the same time. It is created with a combination of UV-filtering and an optical coating similar to a camera lens, which virtually eliminates glare regardless of the distance from the art or objects. This is the most expensive picture framing glass, and it is usually only available from wholesale framing supply distributors or professional picture framers.

Non-glare glass (on the left) has a matte finish, while clear glass (on the right) is shiny.

This valued original art is glazed with museum glass for maximum protection from light damage, but exposure to strong light should still be limited.

Cutting a Sheet of Single-strength Glass

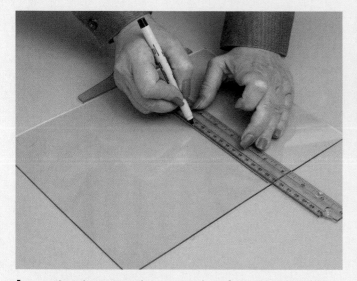

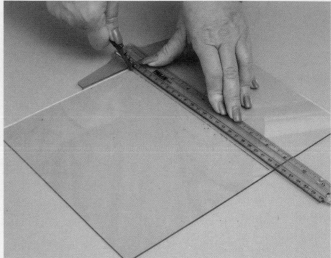

1. Lay the glass on a clean, smooth surface. Stand at the bottom, so the cutter will be pulled toward you. (Some people prefer to begin cutting at the bottom, pushing the cutter toward the top instead of pulling it downward. Practice to find out which is more comfortable.) Measure and mark the cutting point with a permanent marker.

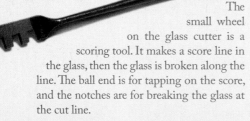

The small wheel on the glass cutter is a scoring tool. It makes a score line in the glass, then the glass is broken along the line. The ball end is for tapping on the score, and the notches are for breaking the glass at the cut line.

2. Align the T-square next to the dot. Place the wheel at the very top of the glass. Be sure to keep it straight up and down, not at an angle.

Pull the cutter along the glass. Use light, steady pressure; tiny bits of glass will appear along the score line, but if there are lots of white chips there is too much pressure. Make one continuous line, letting the cutter run off the glass. Do not retrace the score line, which can damage the cutting wheel and does not improve the score.

3. There are three ways to break the glass along the score line:

a) Align the score line with the edge of the table and snap off the excess.

b) Tap along the score with the ball end of the cutter until the glass breaks.

c) Use glass pliers to grip the glass at the score line and break it.

Cutting Antique Glass

Antique glass is often thick and may contain numerous flaws, especially bubbles. Some people like the look of authentic vintage glass on framing, especially when framing vintage art or photographs. It can be difficult to make a clean cut on antique glass. Sometimes the score breaks clean; other times the cut may be jagged, the glass may refuse to break along the score, or the score may "spider," making cracks in the glass. It is better to use antique glass as it is whenever possible, making the frame fit the glass so it does not require cutting.

Cleaning Glass

Glass has very sharp edges, so extreme caution is required whenever handling it. In areas where glass will be cut, tiny bits of glass will be scattered, so cutting surfaces and floors must be swept often. Even if you will purchase glass in the size needed and won't be cutting it, sharp edges are exposed when cleaning it or placing it in a frame. There are gloves, safety goggles, and lifting tools made to help minimize the danger. Each framer has to determine a practical system for handling glass as safely as possible.

Use an ammonia-free spray cleaner and lint-free cloths or paper towels for cleaning glass.

Mirrors

Pieces of mirror can be purchased by the sheet at home improvement stores or cut to size by a local glass supplier. Ask about thickness: 1/8" (3 mm) thick mirror is not terribly heavy but can have problems with distortion of image, while 1/4" (6 mm) thick mirror offers a stable viewing image but is very heavy. The rabbet of the frame will be reflected into the mirror; color the rabbet with a black marker to conceal the image of raw wood.

Cutting and Cleaning Acrylic

The process for cutting acrylic is similar to the method used for cutting glass, with three differences: A different tool is used, the score can be and often needs to be retraced multiple times, and the break along the score is best made by snapping off the excess. Leave the protective paper on the acrylic throughout the process, until ready to complete the framing.

Cleaning Acrylic

Use mild soap and water or a commercially made plastic cleaner along with a soft, lint-free cloth to clean acrylic.

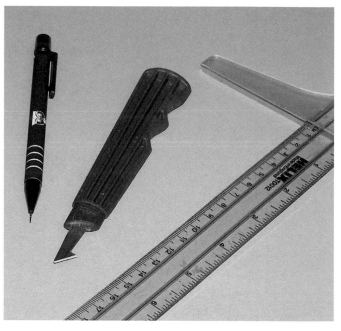

The cutting tool makes a groove in the acrylic with a blade. The acrylic will break along the line of the groove.

Repairing Scratches in Acrylic

Acrylic is easily scratched. Small hairline scratches in acrylic can be rendered nearly invisible by using a commercially made acrylic repair product. Sometimes sold in home improvement stores, and sometimes sold for fixing scratches in plastic eye glass lenses, these products are usually a liquid that is buffed onto the surface to remove tiny debris from the scratch and polish the scratch to a high gloss.

Cutting Acrylic

1. Place the acrylic sheet on a clean, smooth surface. Using a T-square and pencil, measure and mark the cutting line on the protective paper.

2. Align the T-square with the cutting line. Place the scoring tool at the very top of the acrylic, and then pull the tool along the edge of the T-square using firm pressure. It will make a distinctive buzzing sound and produce bits or strings of debris. Repeat the score twice more along the same line to make a deeper groove. Thicker acrylic may require additional scores.

3. Bring the acrylic to the edge of the table, and snap off the excess along the score. Use a craft blade to cut through the back sheet of protective paper to make the separation complete.

THE TOOLS OF THE TRADE

Basic Framing Tools

This basic group of hand tools and supplies is the core of the framing workshop. The assortment a framer needs depends on the type of framing that will be done. It is not important to have every tool or supply; many DIY framers find they need no more than a basic collection of supplies. It is not important to have the exact recommended version of the equipment, but come as close as possible to the primary features of each item. Note: Machines and equipment for building wood frames and cutting mats are discussed in the chapters about those topics.

Picture framing can be done with just a few common hand tools, but for those who plan to do a lot of framing, specialized tools (such as the point driver shown here) make the job much easier.

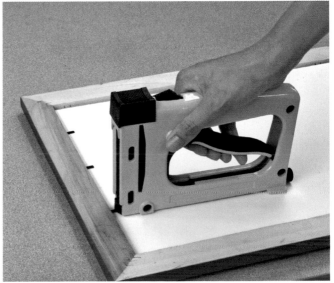

Hand Tools

Most of these are ordinary home workshop tools. The few exceptions are very useful, but not required, for DIY framing.

Hammers. A tack hammer or a small 7-oz. (200 g) claw hammer can be used to build frames, to tap hardware into sectional wooden frame corners, and for fitting wood frames, among other uses.

Screwdrivers. It is good to have a couple of sizes of slotted and Phillips head. Use them to install screws for hanging hardware and to assemble metal frames. Slotted screwdrivers are good prying tools that can come in handy when removing fitting hardware from old frames and when installing or removing spring clips from metal frames.

Pliers. Small is best; some framers even prefer jewelry pliers. Used for pulling wire through loops in hanging hardware, for removing old nails and other hardware from frames, and for various other purposes.

Canvas Pliers. Use for stretching art on canvas and needlepoint.

Staple Gun. Used for attaching oil paintings or needlepoint canvas to a wooden stretcher frame, it can also be used to stretch fabric flat. Use stainless steel staples to avoid future rust. A lightweight craft stapler is fine.

Point Driver. This extremely helpful professional framing tool shoots either round or flat nails (depending on the model) into the rabbet of the frame to hold everything in the frame. This is by far the easiest and neatest method, well worth the investment if numerous

pieces will be framed. It is important to get the correct nail for the driver. Some drivers offer flexible points for work that will be opened often. Point drivers are available from framing supply companies.

Tape Gun. Some framers become comfortable handling loose rolls of double-sided tape; others depend on this type of tape dispenser, which has a trigger to start and stop the tape. It's called an automatic tape gun (ATG) in the framing industry.

Drill. A drill is often needed to start nail holes when building wood frames, and sometimes needed to start screws in hardwood frames for attaching hanging hardware. A basic drill with a few small bit sizes is sufficient.

Wire Cutter. This is used to cut the wire that is strung between screw eyes or D-rings on the back of the frame. A sturdy pair of scissors may do the job but will   dull and chip.

Measuring Tools. Good-quality measuring tools are very important in picture framing, because small measurement errors can make a big difference in the finished framing.

Measuring Tape. Use a metal measuring tape (cloth and plastic can stretch and give inaccurate measurements).

Folding Rule. This extendable ruler (wooden is preferred) is a favorite with professional framers. The most popular size is 6' (1.8 m) long. It may also be called a carpenter's rule.

Ruler. Any clean, smooth ruler will do. Because there is frequent measuring in picture framing, a ruler comes in handy. Picture framers often choose a cork-backed ruler because the cork prevents the ruler from sliding when resting on a smooth surface, such as a matboard.

T-Square. A T-square is useful for checking the squareness of frames and boards, and for marking mats for decorative techniques. For cutting glazing, the size of T-square needed depends on the size of glazing being cut; the T-square must be long enough to run the full length of the cutting line.

Adhesives

Adhesives are an important part of picture framing. They are used to attach mats together, attach art to a backing board, mount fabric to boards, attach backing paper to a frame, and for various other purposes. Using the right adhesive for each purpose is a key part of good framing. The best choice is an adhesive that will remain secure for many years and will do no harm to the art. This eliminates some craft and construction adhesives, which are great for their intended purposes but do not work well in picture framing. Most adhesives needed for picture framing can be found at craft or hobby stores, hardware stores, and home improvement stores locally and online. For strict conservation framing, all attachments that touch the art must be reversible with no adverse effect on the art; these can be found at some craft and hobby stores and from several online sources.

Permanent (#810) and Removable (#811) Magic Tape from 3M

Tapes

Tape may be pressure-sensitive, which means it adheres when pressed to a surface; or water-activated, meaning it must be wetted prior to application. For strictly decorative framing, pressure-sensitive tape is fine, but for valuable art, it is important to use an adhesive that can be safely and completely removed in the future.

Removable Tape. The theory sounds good: The tape is supposed to hold nicely but is easily removable. In practice, this is not a good idea for picture framing, because the hold is not secure enough to be relied on for years, although it can be used to temporarily hold items.

Magic Mending Tape. This is a translucent, matte-finish pressure-sensitive tape from 3M. The polyvinyl adhesive is strong, clean, and acid-free. The ¾" (1.9 cm) width is the most common and most useful.

Mounting Strips/Mounting Corners. These are made specifically for supporting art, with some sort of slot that holds the art and an adhesive backing that mounts the art to a support board. No adhesive makes contact with the art. The types range from ordinary photo corners used to mount photographs in albums or scrapbooks to Mylar strips designed for conservation framing of fine art. Several types are available, but look for one that is acid-free.

Double-Sided Tape. This tape is pressure-sensitive adhesive on both sides of a paper carrier. Rolls of this tape (¼" [6 mm] wide is the favorite) are used for attaching mats together or applying a dust cover to the back of a frame. It's not suitable for contact with art, because it is not removable. Framers typically use an automatic tape gun (ATG) and rolls of tape made to fit the gun, available at some craft stores and from various online sources. The tape can also be applied by hand.

Double-Sided Adhesive. Sold in sheets and rolls, this is a solid layer of adhesive covered on one side or both sides with a release paper. It is used in framing for mounting fabric, decorative paper, or art to a board.

Linen Tape. The type used in picture framing is a strong, conservation-quality cloth with an adhesive backing for attaching heavy paper artwork to a backing board. The adhesive may be pressure-sensitive or water-activated.

Archival Hinging Tape. A lightweight paper coated with an acid-free, water-activated adhesive, this tape is used to attach art to a backing board. It is often called "gummed" tape and is removable with water.

Unsuitable Tapes. DO NOT use masking tape, cellophane tape, packing tape, duct tape, filament tape, or surgical tape anywhere near the artwork. These adhesives dry out, stain, or become too sticky.

Mounting strips and mounting corners from Lineco

Glues

Glues are wet adhesives, which are used for a variety of purposes in picture framing. Many glues are acid-free, but only glues that are fully reversible with water (such as starch paste) should be used in contact with valuable art.

White Glue. This is ordinary white craft glue. It dries clear and strong. It is used for several purposes, such as attaching mats together. Lineco makes a pH-neutral glue that is good for conservation framing purposes.

Fabric Glue. For attaching fabric to a matboard, glue made for fabric can sometimes be better than ordinary white glue, usually because it is thicker and causes less "bleed-through" wetness.

Wood Glue. This glue is used for building wood frames. Specific brands are marketed to picture framers, but hardware and home improvement store versions are fine.

Starch Paste. This is conservation paste used to attach hinges to artwork in conservation framing. Wheat and rice starch are the two most popular in picture framing. They usually come in powder form, to be mixed with water and cooked to a thick consistency, but some types are sold ready to use.

Methyl Cellulose Paste. Another adhesive sold for conservation framing, it comes as a powder that is mixed with cold water when needed, with no cooking required.

Clear Silicone Adhesive. This is a thick, clean, stable adhesive (aquarium sealant or similar) that can be used to attach some objects (such as stone or glass items) to a backing board for shadow box framing. It dries clear and holds strong. It is important to wait for the adhesive to be dried and cured before closing it up in a frame. The package instructions state the cure time, usually twenty-four to seventy-two hours. Objects made of calcium (such as bone or seashells) can be damaged by silicone adhesive, and there are possible interactions with other materials. Dabs of silicone can be peeled away from most nonporous objects if removal is necessary in the future. Do not use construction-grade or any colored type of silicone.

Glue Stick. This is usually a good-quality adhesive that dries clear. Glue sticks can be used for applying dust covers to the backs of frames and for attaching mats together. It is considered a permanent adhesive, although it is briefly repositionable while wet.

Spray Adhesive. For DIY framing, sprays can be useful for full mounting of artwork to a mounting board, but be sure to control the overspray and provide good ventilation. The adhesive usually discolors over time, and the adhesion is not always reliable. It works well for small paper items, but it is unreliable for large posters.

Unsuitable Glues. DO NOT use rubber cement, caulking adhesive, hot melt glue from a glue gun, or other craft glues. All of these adhesives have potentially serious flaws for framing purposes, such as excessive thickness, drying out in a couple of years, or staining everything they touch.

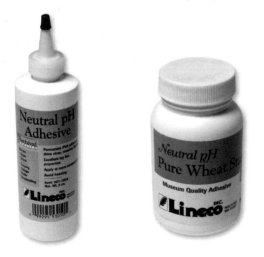

White glue and wheat starch paste powder from Lineco

Boards for Framing: Types and Uses

Matboards were already discussed in Mats and Matboards (page 22), but there are other boards used in framing as well, for backing boards, mounting boards, spacer boards, and filler boards. In conservation framing, it is important to use conservation-quality boards everywhere in the framing.

Backing Board. The backing board is the board directly behind the art. Because the back of the art rests on this board, the quality of the backing board is very significant to the future health of the art. The same is true for mounting boards. If artwork is matted, the backing board is typically a matboard of the same type used for the mat.

Foam Center Board. This versatile board is used for many purposes by picture framers. Lightweight, rigid, and thick, foam center board is basically a compressed sheet of polystyrene with stiff paper adhered to both sides. Ordinary foam center board has a poster board–type of paper. Do not substitute with foam boards made for construction or other industries, which have a crumbly, unstable core. For conservation framing, there is acid-free foam center board with acid-free papers on both sides, and rag foam center board, with 100% cotton paper on both sides. Regular foam center board is available at craft, hobby, and art supply stores, usually with white surface papers and a few other colors. The conservation boards are available mainly online; they have off-white surface papers.

Acid-Free Corrugated Board. This blue-gray board is used as filler board in conservation framing. Do not use it as backing board directly behind art, because the ridges in corrugated board can make marks on artwork. Standard brown corrugated board is highly acidic and should not be used at all in picture framing.

Mounting Boards. Look in art supply departments, craft stores, and online for rigid boards with an acid-free surface, which might be useful for mounting paper or needlework. Illustration boards are very suitable.

Boards for picture framing

Sticky Boards. These are sold in craft and hobby stores and online for mounting artwork and needlework. Some are sticky all over the surface of the board; others have a layer of batting that supports the needlework and a sticky back to hold the excess that is wrapped around the board. Choose a good quality, such as Perfect Mount, which has an acid-free board and pH-neutral adhesive, to avoid possible future damage to the art from acids.

Plywood and Masonite. In rare cases, framers use a sheet of wood as a backing board in a very large frame that may house items that need a lot of support. This significantly increases the weight of the framing, and the acidic wood may need to be sealed, so alternative choices are generally preferred. Fluted plastic sheeting (used by sign shops) or dense foam boards (available from some photography suppliers) may be a better choice.

Unsuitable Boards. Do not ruin an otherwise good frame job by including highly acidic boards that can damage not only the parts of the framing they touch but also other materials in the frame via "acid migration." Poster boards, brown corrugated cardboard, and pressed boards such as those found on the back of tablets of paper are examples of acidic boards that should be avoided in picture framing.

Supplies for Fitting

Fitting refers to the process of finishing the framing: installing all of the materials in the frame, sealing it up, and adding hanging hardware. In addition to the hand tools and nails (or points) needed for fitting, there are a few supplies that can make the job easier or provide beneficial features.

Offset Clips. These metal clips add depth to the frame rabbet to accommodate framing materials that protrude from the frame. They are often used when framing art on canvas. A few different sizes are available to handle different amounts of protrusion. They attach with screws to the back of a frame.

Turn Buttons. These are used to make it possible to open the back of a frame to change artwork as needed. They attach with small screws to the back of a frame. To open the back of the frame, the screws are loosened and the buttons are turned aside.

Canvas Clips. These are narrow, flexible bands of metal made for installing stretcher bars into frames.

FrameSpace. Made to allow space between the glazing and the art in a frame, these acrylic plastic strips provide a slot for the glazing, then a flat expanse of space, and then a ledge for holding the mats, art, and backing. They are available in several sizes, providing from ⅛" (3 mm) to ¾" (1.9 cm) of air space.

EconoSpace. Rectangular acrylic plastic tubes with adhesive on one side, these are used to separate glazing from the mats and art. They are available in several sizes, providing from 1/16" (2 mm) to ⅜" (10 mm) of space.

RabbetSpace. These are specially shaped acrylic plastic strips that attach to the back of a frame with screws. The strips provide extra space, literally extending the depth of the rabbet, for times when the framing materials protrude from the back of the frame. They are available from framing supply companies.

Offset clips

Turn buttons

Canvas clips

EconoSpace from FrameTek

Brown kraft paper on the back of a frame with bumper pads on the lower two corners.

D-rings (strap hangers)

RabbetSpace from FrameTek

Dust Cover Paper. Professional framers complete the back of the frame with backing paper. Some framers use ordinary brown kraft paper, some use black kraft paper for a more sophisticated look, and some use a blue-gray conservation paper made especially for framing. DIY framers sometimes use brown paper bags or suitable wrapping paper.

Hanging Hardware. Screw eyes or ring hardware (D-rings or strap hangers) attach to the two vertical sides of a wood frame. Screw eyes are a loop of metal with a screw attached, which hold wire between them. D-rings are a D-shaped piece of metal attached to a flat piece of metal with one or more holes for screws; they may hold wire or directly hang over hooks on the wall. Sawtooth hangers are narrow bars of metal with a jagged edge that fits over the head of a nail. They are available for wood and metal frames. WallBuddies are triangular metal hardware for hanging large or heavy framing. Adhesive-backed plastic hangers are made to hang art mounted to foam center board. Various sizes of hardware are available to suit the different sizes and weights of frames. Security hangers securely attach art to the wall to discourage theft. Other types of hangers are marketed from time to time. To determine suitability, consider the effect on the wall and the strength needed to hold the framing.

Wire. There are several types of picture frame wire. The most common is braided steel wire, available from hardware stores and craft stores in small packages and online in bigger quantities. There is also plastic-coated wire, which some framers prefer. Choose a wire with a breaking strength about three times the weight of the framing.

Bumper Pads. These felt or plastic pads attach to the two bottom corners of the frame, to keep the frame straight on the wall, provide air circulation, and protect the wall from marks made by the frame. They are optional but very helpful. Most today are made with an adhesive backing, and they simply stick onto the frame or dust cover. Some are made like a tack, with a small metal point that must be tapped in with a hammer.

Easel Backs. These cardboard backings with a hinged stand allow frames to stand up rather than hang on a wall. Available in some stores and from online sources, they are usually associated with photo frames. Most serve as a backing for the frame, but there are some adhesive-backed easels that simply stick to the back of a framed item. Easel backs are suitable for small frames only, usually no larger than 8" × 10" (20.3 × 25.4 cm).

Supplies for Framing Objects and Needlework

Needlework and objects must be attached to a matboard or other support board before framing. A variety of common materials may be used for this purpose.

Supplies for mounting needlework

Thread. Thread is used for mounting needlework and objects. It is available in so many colors, it is almost always possible to find a good match that is nearly invisible when placed next to the work. Use cotton or polyester sewing thread or quilting thread for most purposes. Embroidery floss and silk thread are also options. Some framers like to use clear, plastic monofilament thread, but use polyester thread from the sewing store rather than fishing line. Be careful with monofilament: It can be too sharp for holding fabric, breaking the threads. It can also stretch, so use two or three strands for lasting strength when mounting objects.

Cords. A variety of cords may be used for holding objects in a shadow box. Many types may be used, depending on the needs of the project. The criteria for choosing are strength, attractiveness, and safety of the objects.

Stainless Steel Ballpoint Pins. These are used for stretching needlework using the pinning method. They are sold at stores that sell sewing supplies. The ballpoint tip slides between the fibers of the needlework rather than piercing them, and the stainless steel reduces risk of future rust.

Pins and Needles. For working with needlework and fabric, the framer needs an assortment of ordinary sewing needles, stainless steel ballpoint pins, and some push pins or T-pins.

Cotton Crochet Thread. This strong, thick thread is used for the lacing method of stretching needlework. It is available at craft stores and needlework shops. Other types of sturdy cotton thread may be used. The color is not important, because it will not show in the framing, but most framers use white or cream.

Quilt Basting Tool. This consists of a gun and plastic tabs, very similar to the pricing guns and tags used in clothing stores. It is made for basting the layers of a quilt together to prepare for quilting. Some framers use this tool to attach fabric items, such as t-shirts and sports jerseys to a backing board. Many professional framers think the plastic tabs look awful and prefer the traditional sewing method for mounting clothing and other fabrics.

Mesh Fabric. Fine mesh fabrics such as nylon tulle can be used to wrap objects such as a golf ball or baseball for a nearly-invisible mount in a shadow box.

Fine mesh fabric

Miscellaneous Supplies

All of the items in this section play an important role, depending on the type of framing. Many framers will need only a handful of these items, while some framers will use all of them.

Screws and Nails. The sizes and types depend on the tasks the framer performs. Screws are used to attach D-rings and turn buttons. Tiny nails are used to attach easel backs and sawtooth hangers.

Nail Set 1/32". When building wood frames, this tool is helpful for guiding brads into a frame without making hammer marks on the wood. It is available from hardware and home improvement stores.

Glazier's Push Points. These short points are made to install windows and for other glass installations. They are shorter than brads or framer's points, so they can be useful for installing glass in the rabbet of a shadow box frame when ordinary brads or points would be too long and would show from the face of the frame. They are pushed into the frame with a screwdriver. They are available from hardware and home improvement stores.

Glazier's push points

Nail Hole Filler. The filler used by framers is softer than the type purchased in a regular hardware store. It is a special formula and is available in more than thirty colors to match mouldings from frame supply distributors.

Nail hole filler for picture frames

Awl. A small one is useful for poking holes in matboards when mounting objects, for creating a "starter hole" for screw eyes, and for several other purposes.

Brads (Wire Nails). These are nails with narrow heads. They are used for building wood frames and for fitting framing without a point driver. Some sizes may be available from hardware and home improvement stores. Most are from framing suppliers. A variety of sizes are used, depending on the type of wood. They are sold by length and gauge. The higher the gauge number, the thinner the nail.

Pencil. There is a lot of marking in picture framing, but the ability to erase is important. An ordinary school pencil or a mechanical pencil is best—not too smeary and not too dark.

Erasers. Picture framers like to keep a couple of different kinds on hand for different uses. A white vinyl eraser is a versatile favorite, and a gum eraser can also be useful.

Dusting/ Drafting Brush. A narrow strip of bristles (usually horsehair) attached to a handle, this brush is used to remove dust and debris from glazing and boards before installing in the frame.

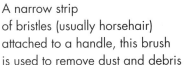

Drafting brush.

Plastic Cutter. This is a handheld tool with a blade for scoring sheets of acrylic.

Safety Goggles. Protective plastic goggles shield the eyes from flying bits of debris in the frame shop, including glass, plastic, wood, and sprays.

Craft Knife and Single-Edge Razor Blades. Trimming a tiny bit of excess from a board, cleaning up a mat opening, cutting tape—there are many uses for a sharp blade that can be easily handled. Craft knives are available with a barrel like a pen, or with a broad handle. Razor blades allow close contact between hand and blade. Choose whichever is most comfortable to handle. Both will be handy.

Glass Cutter. This is a handheld tool with a small wheel for scoring a sheet of glass.

Glass cutter

Glass Pliers. A plastic hand tool, glass pliers are used to break the glass neatly on the scored line.

Glass pliers

Glass Cleaner. Household window cleaners are fine, but look for a minimum of colorant and perfume and no ammonia.

Acrylic Cleaner. Special plastic cleaners are sold, but a mild solution of dish soap and water works fine.

Paper Towels/Cloths. Used for cleaning glass and acrylic, soft and lint-free cloths are best. Cloth rags that can be washed and reused are also useful.

Burnisher/Bone Folder. This tool is used to create firm creases in folded paper or Mylar film, and for burnishing (rubbing). The most popular style is a smooth, flat style. It is used in paper crafts and conservation framing, so it is available from a variety of sources.

Brayer. A smooth rolling wheel on a handle, a brayer is used to burnish adhesives to boards or art to adhesives during several types of mounting.

Squeegee. A firm rectangle of plastic, a squeegee is used to apply pressure to adhere fabric to mats and art to mounting boards, and for other mounting purposes.

Squeegee (in foreground) and two types of brayers

Touch-up Markers. These are made in wood-tone colors specifically for touching up frames. They are also sold in hardware and home improvement stores for touching up furniture.

Touch-up markers from Chartpak

Self-Healing Cutting Mat. This type of mat is sold for many craft purposes, from quilting to scrapbooking. It can be useful in picture framing whenever materials are cut with a craft knife. Thin but very dense, the surface of the mat tolerates repeated cuts without damage and can turn any worktable into a cutting board. It is available in several sizes.

Sandpaper or Emery Boards. Edges on frames and matboards can be smoothed or cleaned with a bit of sandpaper. Ordinary emery boards for manicures generally have an appropriate grit and are easy to handle.

Japanese Paper. Also called rice paper, this is a very strong, thin paper used for making hinges to attach artwork to a backing board in conservation framing. It is available in several weights, from tissue-paper thin to fairly thick: For each project, the hinge paper should be a bit thinner than the art paper. It is available from art supply and conservation framing sources, and also in convenient rolls precoated with water-activated adhesive.

An assortment of Japanese papers

Blotter Paper. In picture framing, this refers to a thick, absorbent cotton paper used to cover conservation hinges while the paste dries. Any heavyweight 100% cotton paper should do, or use two or three layers of thinner cotton paper.

Water. For making paste or wetting tapes in conservation framing, filtered tap water or bottled purified drinking water are recommended by conservators, because minerals that might harm the art have been removed.

Weights. Use something small and clean to hold art still and flat. Glass paperweights are ideal, but some framers make small fabric bags filled with marbles, BBs, or beans; others use polished stones.

Polyester or Polyethylene Film. These are clear, flexible sheets of plastic film. There are several weights available, any of which may be used, as long as it is sufficiently flexible. Called Mylar or Melinex, they can be used for many purposes, including attachments for objects in shadow box framing and encapsulation of paper. Other types of plastic turn yellow, become brittle, and can out-gas chemicals that are unfriendly to artwork. An easy source for polyester or polyethylene film is photo album pages—just make sure the package says the film is made from these materials. Lineco L-Velopes, made from polyester film for storing or framing paper, are sold in stores and online. Mylar is also sold as a graphic arts supply in stores and online, but it may be necessary to purchase an entire roll.

L-Velopes from Lineco

Handy Helpers. In addition to the items listed here, there are a number of useful products available for picture framing that are not necessary but can be very helpful, including tools to help remove spring clips from metal frames, to insert individual brads or points in a frame, and to neatly trim dust cover paper on the back of a frame. A DIY framer can successfully frame pictures for a lifetime without buying any of these, but some framers really enjoy using them.

The SpringMate, PushMate, and PullMate from Fletcher-Terry are made for specific tasks.

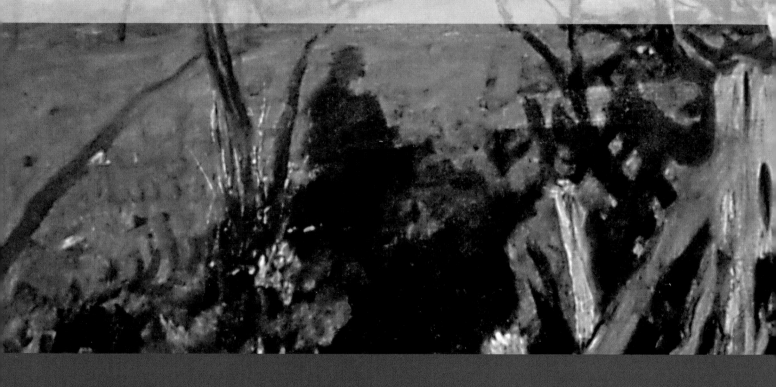

COLOR AND DESIGN

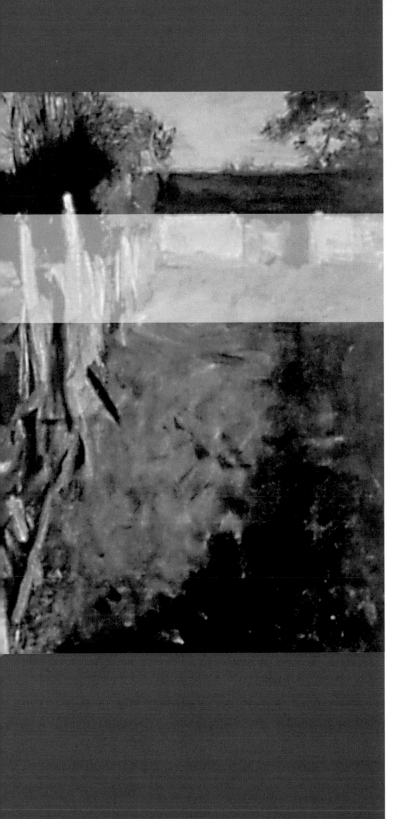

The Basics of Design

Proper construction is essential to the integrity and longevity of picture framing. But framing is made to be looked at, and decisions about color and design determine the success of the visual presentation. Every framed item begins with design. Which frame? What size? What colors? Designing attractive framing does not require great expertise, but it is very helpful to have a general understanding of basic concepts of color and design.

When we discuss color and design concepts as general "rules," there is an implication that something may be done right or done wrong. Well, yes and no. Some of the rules are based on natural law; others are "generally accepted ideas" that are based in cultural traditions. These ideas have a strong following and a long, revered history, and are the basis for many art, design, and architecture classes—hence their status as "rules." Does it matter if we know or follow the rules? It depends: Is the goal to create controversy? To make something odd and edgy? Or to create something pleasing to most viewers? Centuries of tradition combined with recent trends make some things look right and proper to the majority of a culture, while other things look odd and wrong. Learning about the rules gives us a foundation; then we can decide whether or not we wish to follow them.

Even within the boundaries of the rules there is a wide range of possibilities, because we each bring our own point of view to every decision we make about color and design, whether we are buying a teapot or framing a picture. This point of view develops from a combination of our individual life histories and our unique personalities.

Point of view develops from a combination of our individual life histories and our unique personalities.

Very Basic Color Theory

Although personal preference has a lot to do with which colors we think "go together" and which colors we think clash, there is also a science of color that helps us understand the natural connections inherent in the color spectrum.

People have always enjoyed the colors of the rainbow and observed that they always appeared in the same order and blended where they met. In 1666, Sir Isaac Newton used a glass prism to prove that white light is composed of all visible colors, and to advance scientific knowledge of the color spectrum seen in the rainbow. Later the color wheel was developed, as artists gained understanding of the relationship between colors and how colors of paint or dye could be combined to create all colors.

Notice that black and white are not on the color wheel: Black and white are used to create variations, called shades (adding black) and tints (adding white). Adding both black and white creates a tone. A monochromatic color scheme uses tints, tones, and shades from one hue.

This is a typical artist's color wheel with colors arranged in their natural order. Red, blue, and yellow are called primary colors because they are the basis for mixing all other colors. Green, purple, and orange are secondary colors, because they are made by combining two primary colors. The name of a color (red, blue) is referred to as a "hue."

Complementary colors are colors that are opposite one another on the color wheel. Complementary colors are often used together to create a strong contrast that "pops."

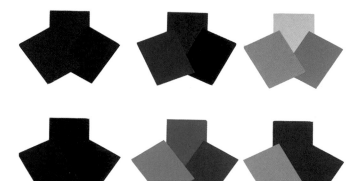

Analogous colors are colors that are close to one another on the color wheel. Use two or three analogous colors to create a harmonious color scheme.

Grays are neutrals created by mixing complementary colors together. Black and white are added to create a range of values (value is the lightness or darkness of a color). Truly neutral grays are rare; most exhibit a hint of the underlying colors they were made from.

What's Your Favorite Color?

If you said blue, you are in good company: Around the world, among both men and women, blue is the most popular color. In a 2000 survey of favorite crayon colors, seven of the top ten were blue. But the other colors have their fans as well, and favorite colors typically change over the course of a lifetime.

Why do we like some colors more than others? As respected color researcher Carlton Wagner says, "Color is in the mind of the beholder as much as it is in the eye." Personal color preferences are developed through life influences and experiences (home region, family life, travel experiences, ethnic background, education), and also through world influences, such as economic conditions, important historical events, and media exposure.

Whether they are aware of it or not, today's average consumer possesses a high level of color sophistication. During the twentieth century, consumers developed an educated color sense, due in part to unprecedented exposure to colorful images, beginning with color motion pictures and magazines, and continuing with television, computer programs, video games, and constant advertising in all visual media.

In survey after survey, blue is the favorite color of both men and women of all ages.

Color Perception

Color perception is an interesting science. Does one person see the same thing as another? We know for certain that some people have impaired color perception, called color blindness. True color blindness—the inability to perceive any colors, so that everything looks like a black and white photo—is extremely rare. The impairment experienced by most color blind individuals can more accurately be described as color deficiency, an inability to perceive the full range of colors. At least 5% of men, and less than 1% of women, are born with color perception deficiencies. Deficiencies in the perception of red and green are by far the most common. The deficient colors are not seen simply as gray; they are rather perceived as distinct colors but very different from the actual colors depicted. Individuals with color blindness can perform all tasks of picture framing except choosing colors of frames, mats, and other colorful parts of the visual framing design.

The actual size of the blue and yellow squares is identical in each example, although they may appear to be different.

Color and Design Trends

Popular trends in picture framing are linked to trends in art, furniture, and home décor accessories. The origin of design trends is somewhat mysterious. Once in a while a full-blown trend emerges from a popular movie, event, or celebrity. More often, the recipe is subtle, composed of numerous ingredients simmering over a period of time. Fashion is one important source, with the youth fashion observed on city streets worldwide providing some of the earliest clues. Graphic arts, seen in print and television ads, and on paper goods such as greeting cards and wrapping paper, are another experimental testing ground. The colors and motifs of world cultures seep into the mix, with different cultures taking center stage depending on world events.

Sometimes color is a significant part of product choice. In fact, color is a factor in most purchases, even when the buyer is unaware of its importance.

Designing Picture Framing

Perhaps the piece you want to frame is a family photo that will join many others on a wall. Or perhaps you are framing an art print that will be the focal point of a dining room wall. Maybe you would like to frame your son's diploma, a vacation postcard, or a watercolor you bought at a local art fair. No matter what type of artwork is being framed, the first step is designing the framing, which includes decisions about color, style, size, and proportion.

Making Choices

When designing the framing for a particular piece of art, there is not just one correct choice. In fact, in most cases, there are numerous attractive ways to frame the artwork. So how do you choose what to use? There are three basic foundations for designing framing:

1. Framing for the Art

This is considered the ideal in picture framing: Select the colors and style of framing based solely on the colors, style, and character of the art. This does not mean you should not use a modern metal frame on an antique print, or an ornate gold frame on a vacation postcard. There is a lot of flexibility and compromise in this ideal. The key principle is to focus on the art. The framing should complement the artwork, creating a harmonious presentation that does not distract the viewer from focusing on the art.

2. Framing for the Room

Framed art can be an essential component of a décor theme, tying various colors and design elements together; artwork is often chosen for that specific purpose. Art and framing intended to integrate with room décor need not be a perfect match with the paint and furniture but should coordinate with it using the same general color palette and style. If the colors and the style of framing do not suit the art at all, it will look out of place, and the visual relationship between the art and its framing will be awkward.

3. Framing for Personal Preference

Your home, your art, your framing, your way. Home décor is an expression of the owner's unique style. A hot pink mat on black and white photos? Absolutely! Ornate Italian frames on vacation postcards from Florida? Why not? Framing that is intentionally offbeat or flashy can be lots of fun, especially in eclectic décor. The goal is to make purposeful design decisions, as opposed to random, uninformed choices. If the completed framing pleases the owner of the framed art, then it is the right choice—no matter how unconventional.

Choosing Colors

Some people think all mats should be white or cream. Others think matting should be more colorful. If color will be important in the framing, using the colors in proportion to how they appear in the art is the general rule: If the picture is mostly blue with a little white and a little pink, a blue mat with a narrow white frame might be best. But a pink mat may be the designer's preference if the art will hang over a pink chair. The first step is to see the colors available in the artwork; in most art, there are many possibilities.

A black and white image usually includes a wide range of grays as well. Sometimes there is no true black or true white at all.

Landscapes often include sky colors, a variety of greens, earth colors, such as brown, and accent colors, such as the red of a barn, offering many options for framing.

What a Difference a Color Makes

In most cases there are numerous color options for frame design, based on the colors in the art. The colors selected from the options to surround the art will affect how the art is perceived. Look at the three examples shown here. All three are appropriate, because all three colors are strongly represented in the photograph—but which looks best?

With a white mat, the yellow and green colors are both strong.

With a green mat, the daffodils really shine.

The yellow mat is a great match for the color of the flowers, but it is so bright it competes with the daffodils for the viewer's attention.

White Mats on Everything?

Over the past few decades, there has been a steady increase in the popularity of white and off-white mats in picture framing, regardless of the colors in the art. Proponents say this creates a neutral environment for any piece of art, which allows the art to stand on its own without distraction. It can help coordinate a collection of framed art that includes a variety of colors and styles. It can make any kind of art look important. The popularity of this style in museums adds to its sophisticated reputation. Of course, as with any design style, opinions differ. Instead of a clean focus on the art, some viewers see a harsh, bright eye-catcher that really does not "go with everything," or they think it is boring! Personal preference based on observation of framed art will determine which opinion seems true.

A white mat allows the colors in the art to have the impact intended by the artist. The designer felt that choosing a mat color from the art would draw too much attention to that individual color.

Using Official Colors

School colors, team colors, academic colors—many organizations and institutions have adopted official colors that become strongly identified with them. Matting is one good way to use official colors in framing, because matting is available in so many colors. Come as close as possible to the correct colors, but don't worry about an exact match—the desired impression will still be created.

Official colors were used in the design of this framing of a diploma from Kent State University.

Putting the Concepts into Practice

Framing for the room narrows the color and style choices to a predetermined range. Look for colors in the art that coordinate with room décor colors, and feature those in the framing design. Framing for the owner's preference is even easier—just do what feels right (of course, plans and decisions are still required).

Framing for the art takes a bit more consideration. It begins with a few simple questions. Look carefully at the artwork: What sort of framing does it want? That may sound strange at first, but it really is not difficult. What colors do you see? Which colors are used a lot? Describe the character— you don't have to be an art expert. Is it bold, bright, pale, serious, rustic, traditional, modern? This character will be your primary focus. Within this focus, find a framing design that also suits your practical needs: Think about where it will hang and what it should accomplish in the room.

Let's follow this process with a couple of pieces of art.

Example 1

Art: Print showing a bathtub

Colors: Pale blue, muted teal, creamy yellow, white

Character: The style is realistic, but a texture shows clearly in the print, giving the piece a weathered appearance. The colors are soft. It could be old-fashioned or contemporary, depending on the framing.

Goal: This print will be part of a coastal décor theme in a bathroom, which will include seaside-related accessories, such as shells and coral. It will hang on a pale blue wall over a cream sink with a beige counter. The wood in the room is painted white.

Framing Options: A white frame would show nicely on the blue wall and would coordinate with the wood in the room. Silver metal would be fine if the fixtures are chrome. A blue frame could help bring out the blue in the art but could overwhelm the art if too big or too bright. All of the colors in the painting are potential mat colors, although white or beige, perhaps with a hint of blue in a double mat, might be best for the room.

Example 2

Art: Lighthouse print

Colors: A range of browns, plus red, blue, off-white, and black

Character: The colors, style, and subject matter are traditional in a folk art vein. The map border may be used in the framing or may be covered by a mat.

Goal: This print will hang in a home office. The walls are off-white and most of the furniture is reddish cherry. The only other art in the room is a poster-size map of the world in a brass metal frame. The lighthouse print will have a large space to itself on the wall.

Framing Options: A brass frame to match the other frame is one option, but a cherry wood frame would also suit the art and room. The print could be framed with no mat, but a mat would expand the size and allow the art to fill a bigger space on the wall. An off-white mat with a cherry frame would be fine, but it would also be attractive to use an antique red or warm brown mat with a brass frame.

Size and Proportion

Choosing the colors for framing is the first step. Then the shape and size of the design must be determined. Some framers make rules for themselves, such as using 3" (7.6 cm) of matting on any art that is 16" × 20" (40.6 × 50.8 cm) or larger. A better method is to design framing for each individual project, based on the art and the goals of the framing.

One general guideline of design tells us to vary the size of different elements of framing, because sameness can cause a lack of focus. For example, if the mat is 2" (5.1 cm) wide, the frame should be 1" (2.5 cm) wide or 2½" (6.4 cm) wide, but not 2" (5.1 cm) wide.

Proportion is a relationship between the shape, size, and position of different elements in a design. Good proportion is achieved when the design is "balanced." How does one measure balance and find good proportion? This is one of those "rules" discussed at the beginning of the chapter, with western culture generally preferring symmetry and equal division of space. Ultimately, it is a matter of personal perception.

Rectangular mats and frames are generally used on oval art prints to balance the proportion without distracting from the art.

Which looks best? Does the art look crowded or comfortable?

The proportions of the mat and frame were varied to achieve a good balance.

Similar size art can be made into a matching set of same-size frames by adjusting the mat opening and the amount of matting that surrounds each art image. This involves varying proportions, but the results are usually acceptable.

A Note about Frame Styles

When we speak of style in framing, we are talking about the overall character of the finished piece. It may be formal, modern, romantic, or playful. There may be some natural connection between the art and framing, such as a bamboo frame and scroll-style mat on an Oriental watercolor. Or the style of the frame may match the character of the art, such as a rough wood frame in driftwood gray on a stormy beach scene. Refer to the chapters about matting (page 22) and frames (page 14) to examine some of the typical styles.

Want to use historic frame styles on historic art? It is easy to do a bit of research online or at the library to find out what type of framing is historically accurate. This may be as simple as a plain, rustic frame on an early American needlework or a black and gold Hogarth frame on an antique print.

Most often, the style of frame is chosen without regard to history, and many frames are designed the same way, mingling design styles of many cultures and time periods to create versatile mouldings that will suit many types of art. Most designers are guided by the style of the art, the style of the room where the art will hang, or a combination of both.

The Eiffel Tower and the Art Nouveau–style frame are a historic match: Both represent exciting new designs in France at the turn of the twentieth century.

Designs with Multiple Images

Sometimes numerous photographs or objects are displayed together in one frame. With multiple objects, the goal is to avoid crowding (too little space between items), but make sure the objects relate to one another in the design—too much empty space between items creates a "disconnected" look. The right spacing is not a matter of mathematical precision; in a frame containing numerous items it often looks better if the spacing is varied rather than identical. Finding the right balance is a matter of trial and error: Try different arrangements of multiple objects until a suitable arrangement is found. Once the arrangement has been determined, add a mat border larger than the space between items to bring focus to the images. An example is to use 1" (2.5 cm) between the images and a 2" (5 cm) border surrounding all the images.

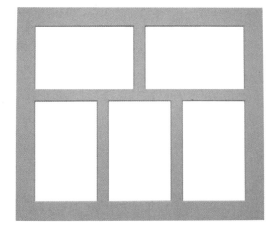

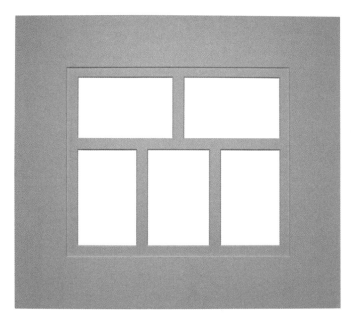

Ready-made mats with multiple openings are sold to display a collection of items, usually photographs. To make a less crowded, more elegant presentation, a larger, single-opening mat may be placed on top of the first mat. Notice how changing the matting changes the character of the presentation.

The Size and Weight of Artwork

There is tremendous freedom of choice when designing framing, but there are a few important restrictions that may be imposed by the art or objects that will be framed. In short, the frame must be deep enough and strong enough to securely hold the items it will house.

The frame should be deep enough to completely contain all of the layers of framing materials. An "overfill" of ⅛" (3 mm) or ¼" (6 mm) can be overcome with a couple of framers' tricks, but after that the bulk becomes unmanageable and the protrusion looks odd when hanging on the wall. Stuffing the frame will cause buckling of paper and boards over time.

Wood frames require substantial width or depth to be very strong. A narrow, ½" (1.3 cm) deep wood frame will not successfully hold a full-size poster with glass: The frame may twist during handling, breaking the glass, or the bottom corners of the frame will fail within a short time, or the hanging hardware (which will have a weak and insufficient installation) will pull out of the frame and the whole thing will fall to the floor. Metal sectional frames are strong for their size, but there is a limit. There are no hard and fast rules for choosing a strong enough frame, but it is an important consideration whenever the framing materials are heavy, or the project is large.

This frame is appropriate for the size and weight of the framing materials it holds.

There are ways to compensate for a slightly "over-filled" frame, but it is best to choose a frame that is deep enough to hold all of the framing materials.

DOING THE MATH IN PICTURE FRAMING

Understanding fractions is an important part of picture framing. Artwork must be measured carefully, and mats and frames must be made the correct size, with very little room for error. This ruler shows ½, ¼, ⅛ and ⅟₁₆ of an inch.

The Importance of Accurate Measuring

Careful, accurate measuring is one of the most important parts of successful picture framing. When it comes to measuring art and determining mat and frame sizes, working with fractions is an important part of the process. Lots of people, including picture framers, find working with fractions a bit aggravating, but with a little practice it becomes routine.

If you are simply not a math person, some of the exercises in this chapter may seem a little confusing, but be assured that they will quickly make sense once they are applied to actually cutting a mat.

Use a good-quality ruler, carpenter's rule, or metal measuring tape for measuring. Use only pencil to record measurements to avoid permanent marks on artwork and mats. Also be careful not to make dents or scratches on the surface of the art with the measuring tool. Even bright color nail polish can make a mark on the artwork, if the edge of a fingernail swipes along the art.

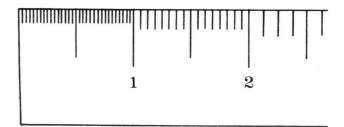

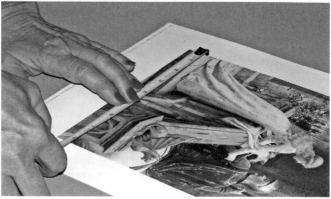

The full sheet of paper measures 11" × 14" (27.9 × 35.6 cm), but the image alone measures 8" × 10" (20.3 × 25.4 cm).

Measuring Art that Will Not Be Matted

Needlework, art on canvas, some art prints, and photographs may be framed without matting. If glazing will be used, remember that space between the art and the glazing is important.

Lay the art flat. Use weights, if necessary, when measuring artwork that has been rolled in a tube. Measure the art image in both directions. For art on paper, this may be the entire sheet of paper, or just a portion of it. Measure at the approximate center, both horizontally and vertically. Most paper reproductions will be square, but you can never be sure. Remember the lip of the frame will cover the edges of the art on all four sides.

For needlework, blocking or pressing may be necessary before measuring. Determine the exact image size, remembering that the lip of the frame will cover ¼" (6 mm) on all four sides.

For a stretched canvas, the size of the bars and the thickness of the canvas wrapped around the bars may add fractions of an inch to a "standard" size. Check to see if the canvas is square—an "out-of-square" canvas may measure smaller at one corner than another.

Measuring Art that Will Be Matted

Most art on paper (such as prints, drawings, photographs, and watercolor paintings) and many needlework pieces will be matted. The mat must overlap the art a minimum of ⅛" (3 mm) on each side, and a bit more is even better—otherwise the art can peek through or even fall through the mat opening if the frame is jostled or during changes in heat and humidity. If the image has extra blank paper around it, it is still important to cover a bit of the image with the mat, or any error in mat cutting will result in unwanted blank paper showing within the mat opening. Either measure the art exactly and subtract ¼" (6 mm), or simply measure slightly short of the edges of the image. Of course, more of the art can be covered if desired to hide dirt, holes, or other unwanted portions of the image.

This is a typical 8" × 10" (20.3 × 25.4 cm) photograph. The mat opening for this photo will be 7¾" × 9¾" (19.7 × 28.8 cm), allowing the mat to cover the photo ⅛" (3 mm) on all four sides.

Alternative Mat Openings

The mat does not always cover the edges of the art. Here are some examples.

Print Paper as a Border

Many art prints have at least a couple of inches (centimeters) of extra paper surrounding the printed image; it is typically white. This can serve as a border if desired. Measure the art image exactly, and then add the amount of paper that will show in the mat opening, usually between ¼" (6 mm) and ¾" (1.9 cm) on all four sides.

Engravings and Other Art with a Plate Mark

A plate mark is a raised or indented rectangle on the art paper where a printing plate made an impression, or where an artificial plate mark was created. It is customary to show the plate mark in the mat opening.

Limited Edition Prints

It is common practice to show the signature on a limited edition print, and the signature is most often on the blank paper just below the image, in the right corner. If the print is numbered, the numbering is commonly at the left with the title in the center. When measuring the art, include enough of the blank paper at the bottom to include the entire signature. For balance, some blank paper should be shown on the other three sides as well: either the same amount as was shown at the bottom, or a smaller amount, such as ¼" (6 mm) or ½" (1.3 cm). This choice is a matter of personal preference.

Floated Art

Floated art is suspended on the backing board with all of the edges of the art showing. The backing board becomes part of the framing design, acting as the first border of color around the art. A window mat is usually added. The opening for the window mat may be just ¼" (6 mm) away from the edges of the art, or it may be 1" (2.5 cm) or more if preferred. Carefully measure the art, and then add the amount of backing board that should show to determine the mat opening.

Mat Mathematics

To determine the outside size of a mat, the mat borders are added to the mat opening. Remember that the total of two borders must be added to each dimension: Both the top and bottom borders must be added to the vertical measurement of the mat opening, and both the left and right borders must be added to the horizontal measurement of the mat opening. This may sound obvious, but forgetting this is one of the most common mistakes made by inexperienced framers.

1. Measure the artwork and determine the opening for the mat.

2. Add the amount of both side borders (left side and right side) to the horizontal opening measurement.

3. Add the amount of both the top and bottom borders to the vertical opening measurement.

4. The total will be the outside size of the mat, and the size of the backing board, filler board, and glazing. The frame will be just a bit larger, so the materials can fit comfortably in it.

Let's look at a couple of examples:

The artwork is vertical and measures 16" × 20", so the mat opening will be 15¾" × 19¾".

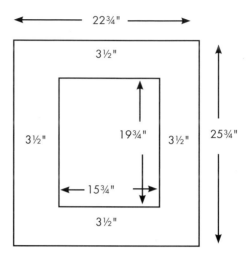

Adding equal mat borders.

Opening size

15 ¾" × 19 ¾"

+ 7"   7" (3½" each side)

22 ¾" × 26 ¾" (outer size of the mat)

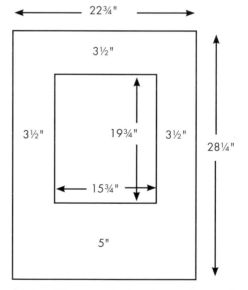

Adding different mat borders. (extra at bottom for a museum style mat)

Opening size

15 ¾" × 19 ¾"

+ 7"   8 ½" (3 ½" top and sides, 5" bottom)

22 ¾" × 28 ¼" (outer size of the mat)

Determining the Size of a Double Mat

A double mat is two mats stacked together, with a small amount of the bottom mat exposed within the window of the top mat. This is done by cutting two different size openings: one for the liner mat, another for the top mat. The exposed part of the bottom mat is called a lip, liner, or reveal. The reveal is typically ¼" (6 mm) wide, but it may be ⅛" (3 mm) or some other amount.

When cutting a double mat, the bottom mat border is the full size of the mat border the designer has chosen. If the designer selects a 3" (7.6 cm) mat border, the liner mat will be 3" on all four sides. The top mat must be cut with a larger opening, to reveal some portion of the liner mat; a larger mat opening means a smaller amount of mat border for the top mat. The amount of decrease in the size of the top mat border is determined by the size of the reveal. If the bottom mat reveal will be ¼" (6 mm) on all four sides, subtract ¼" (6 mm) from the full border size. In our example, 3" (7.6 cm) minus ¼" (6 mm) equals a 2¾" (7 cm) top mat border.

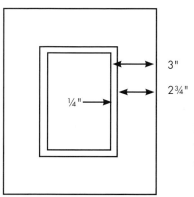

Mat Borders for a double mat
Total mating: 3"
Top mat border: 2¾"
Liner mat: ¼"

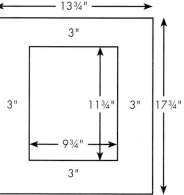

"Rounding" the mat borders
The artwork is 8" × 12" vertical
Original size of mat

Designing Mats to Fit Ready-Made Frames

"Rounding" Measurements

If the outer mat size is close to a standard size, the mat border can be made a little bit bigger or smaller to allow the use of a ready-made frame. For example, the mat for an 8" × 12" (20.3 × 30.5 cm) print will have an opening size of 7¾" × 11 ¾" (19.7 × 29.8 cm) (allowing the mat to cover ⅛" [3 mm] of the art on all four sides). The designer wants a 3" (7.6 cm) mat border on each side, so the outside size of the mat will be 13¾" × 17¾" (33.6 × 45 cm). If ⅛" is added to each mat border (3⅛" [7.9 cm] instead of 3" [7.6 cm]), the mat size will be 14" × 18" (35.6 × 45.7 cm), which is a standard size for ready-made frames. The slightly larger mat border will make little difference in the appearance of the mat, but it can make the project easier to complete.

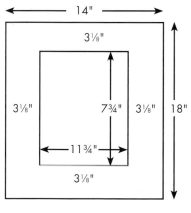

Mat border "rounded up"

Adjusting the Fit

Often, the fit is not that convenient, and the art does not fit into a standard size with equal mat borders on all four sides. There are two ways to compensate: Change the mat opening to cover more of the art where needed, or allow the mat to have unequal borders. Both are acceptable solutions.

Option 1: Change the Opening

The art measures 15" × 20" horizontally. The ready-made frame measures 20" × 24". The typical mat opening would be 14¾" × 19¾", leaving 5¼" available for matting at the top and bottom, and 4¼" available for the sides. The designer looks at the art, which is a landscape, and decides that an additional 1" of the grassy hill on the right side could be covered by the mat without doing any harm to the presentation of the image. The new mat opening is 14¾" × 18¾", which leaves a total of 5¼" available for matting on all four sides. Each mat border will be one half of 5¼", or 2⅝".

Option 2: Don't Change the Opening

The art measures 15" × 20" horizontally. The ready-made frame measures 20" × 24". The typical mat opening would be 14¾" × 19¾", leaving 5¼" available for matting at the top and bottom, and 4¼" available for the sides. The designer looks at the art, which is a photograph, and decides all of the image is important and should not be covered (except for the necessary ⅛"). The mat can be cut in two possible styles:

Version A—Allowing Uneven Mat Borders: The matting can be divided equally (5¼" divided by 2 equals 2⅝" for the top and bottom mat borders, 4¼" divided by 2 equals 2⅛" for the mat border on the two sides).

Version B—An Extended Bottom Border: The designer may prefer to use an extended bottom mat border, which is a popular style. The side borders will be divided evenly (4¼" divided equally between the two sides, or 2⅛"). The top mat border will also be 2⅛", so it will use 2⅛" of the 5¼" that are available. To determine the bottom border, subtract 2⅛" from 5¼", which equals 3⅛".

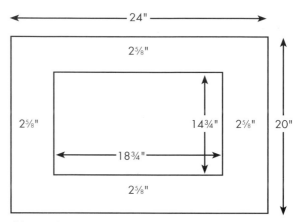

Change the opening

Adjusting the fit of the mat. The art is 15" × 20" horizontal. The frame is 20" × 24"

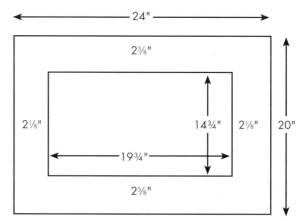

Version A: Allowing uneven mat borders

Option #1. Don't change the opening. Divide border equally.

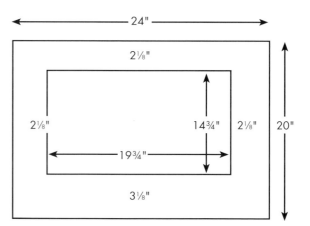

Version B: An extended bottom border

Option #2. Don't change the opening. Three sides equal, extra bottom.

Designing a Double-Opening Mat

This is a simple addition process—just make sure all of the measurements are included in the addition.

Example: Two vertical 5" × 7" photos (each opening 4¾" × 6¾") are going to be framed together, side-by-side. The designer wants 1" of matting between the two photos, and 2" of mat border on all four outer borders.

The horizontal size is $\quad$ 4¾" + 4¾" + 1" + 2" + 2" = 14 ½"

(Photo 1 width + photo 2 width + 1" of matting between the photos + 2" of mat on the left side + 2" on the right)

The vertical size is $\quad$ 6¾" + 2" + 2" = 10 ¾"

(The vertical photo size + 2" of mat on the top border + 2" on the bottom border)

The outer mat size is $\quad$ 10¾" × 14½"

This is close to a standard size: 11" × 14". To make the mat 11" × 14", the top and bottom borders can be 2⅛", and the side borders 1¾", or the mat openings for the photographs can be 4¼" × 6½", with a 2¼" border on all four sides.

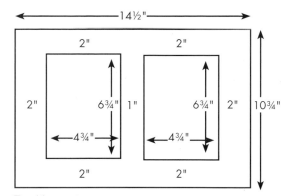

Double opening mat

Two photographs, each 5" × 7" vertical. Original plan for opening and mat borders

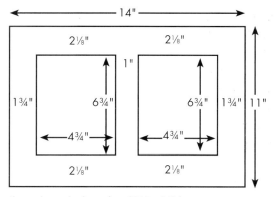

Change the mat borders to fit and 11" × 14" frame

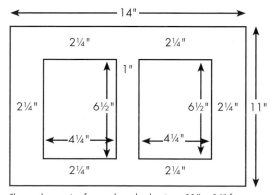

Change the opening for equal mat borders in an 11" × 14" frame

CUTTING MATS

Choosing Equipment

A mat can be cut using a craft knife with a fresh blade (art students do it quite often) but the results are not satisfactory for mats that will hang in a home or office. No matter how much time and care is taken, the cuts are usually uneven and/or ragged. The cuts are straight up and down, and a clean, beveled cut is one of the most important features of professional-looking matting. Even an untrained observer is likely to notice a rough mat opening. The DIY framer who anticipates cutting mats on a regular basis needs to purchase a mat cutter that will provide that clean beveled cut. If mats will be cut infrequently, or the DIY framer is not yet ready to make an investment in framing equipment, ready-made mats or mats cut at a custom framing shop are good alternatives.

A distinct bevel is the standard for professional framing; it can also be the standard for DIY framers.

Choosing Equipment

A variety of good-quality mat cutters is available for the DIY framer, from a basic, no-frills setup to a professional version. Some DIY framers use the basic model quite successfully to cut a large number of mats. Others enjoy the features of the more advanced models even though they only cut mats occasionally. Each framer must determine what is best, but remember: Mat cutting is a skill, and practice is important no matter which equipment is chosen.

The Logan Craft & Hobby mat cutter uses a handheld, push-style cutting head and cuts mats with an outer size up to 23½" (60 cm).

Examples of Equipment

Most mats are cut with straight lines for both the outer shape and the openings, so sometimes mat cutters are referred to as "straight line mat cutters." A separate machine is required for cutting ovals and circles; this is discussed on page 84.

Handheld Cutter. A favorite with art students, the handheld mat cutter can cut an opening in a matboard, and even provides a bevel, but it takes a lot of practice to do it well. However, this tool is inexpensive and readily available from craft and art supply stores, and can be an entry-level mat cutter for the beginner DIY framer. The instructions in this chapter use a more professional style of mat cutter, but all of the mats can be cut using a handheld cutter if preferred. Use a T-square and pencil to draw the cutting lines.

This DIY mat cutter (Logan 301 Compact) comes with a straight cutting head and a bevel cutting head. It cuts boards with an outer measurement of up to 32" (81 cm). A glass cutting head is also available.

Handheld Cutter with a Base. This is a big improvement on the handheld cutter used alone. It provides a sturdy base and a bar that guides the cutting head. With practice, a DIY framer can cut any type of straight line mat with this practical system.

Professional-style Mat Cutter. This type of cutter has a solid base that holds a cutting head that slides along a metal bar. Several sizes are available to suit the needs of different framers; the size of a mat cutter refers to the length of the mat it can cut. This machine is great for a DIY framer who cuts a lot of mats.

Stops for Mat Cutters. These devices, also called "measuring stops" or "production stops," attach to a mat cutter and let the framer know exactly where the cutting line should stop, without any pencil marks. They are available for some DIY cutters.

This professional style mat cutter (Logan 750 Simplex Plus) has the features and accessories that professionals use, including stops and a squaring arm for trimming boards to size before cutting a mat. It is available in two sizes, 40" and 60" (102 cm and 152.5 cm) capacity.

Tips for Cutting Mats

Regardless of the equipment chosen for cutting mats, there are some simple tips that will increase the chances of consistent success.

Sharp Blades. Dull blades cause many problems when cutting mats. It is better to spend pennies on a fresh blade than to spend dollars on a new matboard. How many cuts can be made before the blade is too dull? This depends on the dampness and density of the board, which varies.

Dry Boards. Dry boards make good mats, while damp mats are a source of trouble. Avoid storing or cutting boards in a humid environment.

Equipment Tests. Practice on scrap matboard to check the sharpness and length of a blade before cutting a mat.

Pencil. An ordinary graphite pencil is the only marking tool that should be permitted where mats are marked and cut. Light pencil marks are easily erased from most matboards, which is not true for pens or markers.

Slip Sheet. Use a slip sheet for all bevel cuts. It will provide a nice smooth cut because it holds the face of the matboard tight to the surface when the blade is inserted and pulled through.

Blade Depth. The blade depth is very important; the blade should cut through one sheet of board and scratch the surface of the slip sheet. If the blade is extended too far it will cause irregular cuts.

Trimming Boards to Size

The first step in cutting a mat is accurately trimming a matboard to the outer size of the mat. Squareness is essential or the mat borders will not be straight and aligned. Boards can be trimmed on a self-healing cutting mat with a utility knife (sharp blade, please) or in a straight line mat cutter. A standard matboard measuring 32" × 40" will typically be fractionally larger than 32" × 40" because the board must travel to different climates and may shrink slightly due to temperature and humidity changes. It is made larger to ensure a full 32" × 40" is available for cutting. If you cut a 32" × 40" into four 16" × 20" pieces, each board will be fractionally smaller.

Do not assume the outer edges of a purchased matboard are square—check to make sure, and trim the board if necessary.

The Slip Sheet

A slip sheet is a strip of scrap matboard placed beneath a mat while the bevel opening is being cut. The slip sheet receives the tip of the blade during each cut, creating a smoother cut. A slip sheet is usually between 5" (12.7 cm) and 10" (25.4 cm) wide, but it must always be a few inches (centimeters) wider than the mat border, and it should be at least a couple of inches (centimeters) longer than the largest dimension of the mat.

Most framers get a much cleaner cut when they use a slip sheet while cutting a mat.

Cutting a Single Mat

Let's start with a basic, single mat. The cutter used here (the Logan Simplex model) is the "pull" type, meaning the cut starts at the top of the cutter and runs toward the framer.

1. Cut a matboard to the exact outside measurements. Set the mat guide on the cutter to the correct border size. In this example, the matboard is 9" × 11" (22.9 × 27.9 cm) and will have a 2" (5.1 cm) border, creating a 5" × 7" (12.7 × 17.8 cm) opening.

2. Stand at the bottom of the cutter and lift the bar. Insert a slip sheet. Place the matboard face down on the slip sheet.

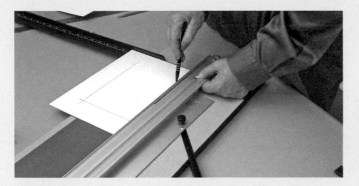

3. Hold the matboard firmly against the edge of the mat guide and flat against the bottom rule. Using a pencil, draw a line that will act as a guide for the cutting head. Draw lightly on all four sides, overlapping the lines at the corners. The intersecting lines show where to start and stop the cut.

4. Place the right hand on the cutter head. Slide the cutting head up to the top of the mat. Press down to insert the blade just slightly above the intersection. The cutter in the example has a white line to guide the placement of the blade.

5. Hold the head tight and pull toward you. Continue until just slightly past the intersection line (or until the guide line reaches the intersection). Cutting beyond the intersection creates overcuts, which are visible on the face of the mat.

6. Lift the handle slightly with the left hand while turning the matboard to the next side with the right hand, then cut the second side as the first.

7. Continue around the four sides. When the fourth side of the mat is cut, the center piece of board will be released. This piece is called the fallout or dropout. It can sometimes be discarded or used for another framing, but sometimes it is needed, as when cutting a double mat.

8. The finished mat.

Troubleshooting

If the fallout is not released, there are "short cuts" on the mat, meaning the cut is not complete at the corners. Do not remove the fallout, or the unfinished corners will tear. Instead, slip a single-edge razor blade into the cut through the face of the mat, at the same angle as the cut, and finish the cutting to the corner.

Even a pro can make a rough cut from time to time, but many minor problems can be repaired. A craft knife can trim extra bits at the corners, and light strokes with an emery board can clean up ragged, uneven spots along the bevel.

Mats with Different Borders

To cut a mat that has different mat borders (such as 2" [5.1 cm] on the sides and 3" [7.6 cm] on the top and bottom), all four corner intersections must be marked before cutting. Measure and mark (with pencil) using a T-square or the mat cutter. Then cut the mat, setting the cutter twice (at 2" [5.1 cm], then at 3" [7.6 cm]) to cut the two different sizes of borders, using the marks to indicate where each cut starts and stops. It can be helpful to label the mat with the border widths.

Cutting a Reverse-Bevel Mat

For some purposes it looks better if the mat has no visible bevel; mats that will have a fillet moulding installed in the window opening are one good example. Mats that will be covered with fabric are another example. To make a reverse bevel on a mat opening, the mat is cut face up instead of face down. Be careful to avoid overcuts at the corners, and make sure pencil marks are light and easily erased. Note: If your mat cutter can make a straight cut in addition to a bevel cut, it is fine to use the straight cut with a fillet or fabric-covered mat; this mat may be cut face up or face down.

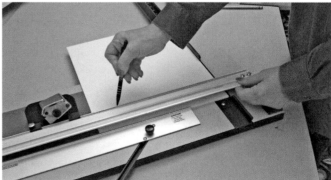

Cutting a Double Mat

A double mat is literally two mats on top of one another, cut with different openings so that a narrow lip of the bottom mat is exposed in the opening of the top mat. This is the most popular mat in professional framing, because it gives a finished presentation to almost all types of artwork, and because the second layer of matboard provides a little extra space in the frame, which is beneficial for the art.

Because only a small amount of the bottom mat will show, some framers try to use a small piece of matboard, just a bit bigger than the opening of the top mat. This is a poor practice that may save pennies but can cause trouble in the future. Skimping on the board directly on top of the art weakens the support needed for stability of the framing package. Uneven layers will cause buckling of the materials in the frame.

The two boards for a double mat can be cut separately. That is, two pieces of board can be cut to the outer size of the mat. Then one board is cut using the liner opening, the other is cut using the top mat opening, and the two are put together.

Here's an example: The outside of the mat is 14" × 18" (35.6 × 45.7 cm) with a 3" (7.6 cm) border, and ¼" (6 mm) of liner mat will be revealed on all four sides. This means the bottom mat will have a 3" (7.6 cm) border and the top mat will have a 2¾" (7 cm) border (3" minus ¼" [7.6 cm minus 6 mm]).

Trim two boards, one in the top mat color, one in the liner mat color, to 14" × 18" (35.6 × 45.7 cm). Cut the liner mat with a 3" (7.6 cm) border. Cut the top mat with a 2¾" [7 cm] border. Align the top mat on the bottom mat. Attach the two together using white glue or double-sided tape.

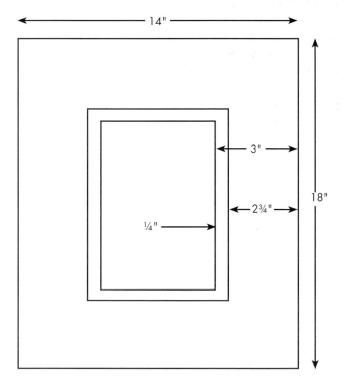

Cutting the two mats separately. The narrow inner lip of a double mat allows the designer to use a small amount of an accent color that enhances the art.

Cutting the Perfect Double Mat

When the two parts of a double mat are cut separately, the two mats do not always align perfectly, because of minor shifts in the boards during cutting. In this method, the two mats are attached to one another during cutting of the liner mat. The top mat is cut first, serving as a template for the liner mat, so the two mat openings are perfectly aligned. The board for the liner mat is cut slightly smaller than the top mat, so that the edges of the liner board will not interfere with the edges of the top board during cutting.

This example will create an 5" × 8" (12.7 × 20.3 cm) opening in an 11" × 14" (27.9 × 35.6 cm) mat. The total mat border will be 3" (7.6 cm) on all sides, making a 2¾" (7 cm) top mat with a ¼" (6 mm) liner revealed.

1. Trim the top matboard to 11" × 14" (27.9 × 35.6 cm). Cut a 2¾" (7 cm) border in this mat. Save the fallout from the center of the mat.

2. Trim the bottom board to 10¾" × 13¾" (27.3 × 34.9 cm). Apply a short piece of double-sided tape to all four sides of the surface of the bottom mat. Adhere the top mat to the bottom matboard with the face of the bottom matboard against the back of the top mat.

3. Apply a small strip of double-sided tape to the back of the fallout piece, and replace it in the mat opening, pressing to adhere it to the bottom matboard. The fallout creates a level cutting surface and also serves as a slip sheet

4. Remove the slip sheet. Set the double board unit face down in the cutter. Set the cutter for a 3" (7.6 cm) border. Cut all four sides. The fallout will drop away, leaving an even, perfectly aligned double mat.

Design Tip

A triple mat can be cut the same way by cutting a third piece of matboard, attaching it to the double layer mat and fallout, and cutting a wider mat border. As a general rule of design, it is best to vary the size of the lines surrounding the art. For example, if the innermost liner reveals ½" (1.3 cm) of color, the next liner might reveal ¼" (6 mm).

Cutting a Double-Opening Mat

This mat is usually made for a matched pair of items, such as two photo portraits, or a set of art prints. Careful measuring and marking of cutting lines is the key to a successful double-opening mat. The top, bottom, and side borders of the mat can be cut using the ordinary settings on the mat cutter, but pencil marks will indicate where to start and stop. Because there are two separate openings, the cutting line will not be continuous from corner to corner; it will be interrupted by a strip of matting between the two openings. The fourth side of each opening, at the interior of the mat, will be guided by pencil marks alone.

This example is for framing two vertical 5" × 7" (12.7 × 17.8 cm) photos in an 11" × 14" (27.9 × 35.6 cm) horizontal frame. The opening for each photo will be 4¼" × 6½" (10.8 × 16.5 cm). The designer has chosen to have 1" (2.5 cm) of mat between the two photos. There will be 2¼" (5.7 cm) of mat border on all four sides.

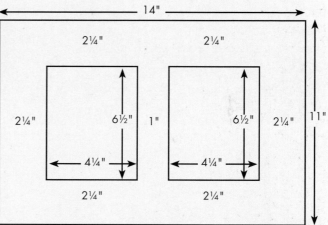

Change the opening for equal mat borders in an 11" x 14" frame

1. Using a T-square and pencil, draw all of the corner intersections for both openings.

2. Set the mat cutter at 2¼" (5.7 cm) and cut the outer mat borders, using the pencil marks to start and stop at the strip of matting between the two openings.

3. There are two remaining cuts to make—the interior cuts. Slide the mat guide out of the way or remove it if necessary. Insert the mat in the cutter aligned with the pencil marks of the interior side of one mat opening. Be careful—it is easy to get confused and cut this fourth side with the bevel facing the wrong way! Flip the mat around, and cut the fourth side of the second opening.

Cutting an Oval Mat

Cutting oval or circle mat openings requires a separate cutting machine, usually a simple, portable apparatus. An oval mat cutter will also cut an oval shape for the outer measurement, if necessary, to fit in an oval frame. This type of cutting will take a bit of practice.

The two settings on a portable mat cutter work on the "differential" principal: the difference between the width of the mat opening and the height of the mat opening. For example, to cut a 5" × 7" (12.7 × 17.8 cm) oval opening in a mat, one scale is set at 5" (12.7 cm) and the other at 2" (5.1 cm), which is the difference between 5" and 7" (12.7 and 17.8 cm). This creates an oval of the desired shape. To make a circular opening, the first scale is set to the width of the opening, and the second scale is set at 0", because there will be no difference between height and width. Oval and circle mats are cut face up. Depending on the cutting machine, the opening may have a straight cut or a bevel cut.

This example will make a 5" × 7" (12.7 × 17.8 cm) oval opening in an 8" × 10" (20.3 × 25.4 cm) rectangle.

The Logan Oval and Circle Mat Cutter (#201)

1. Cut an 8" × 10" (12.7 × 17.8 cm) piece of matboard. Carefully measure and mark the center of the board; accuracy is very important to the position of the oval opening. Mark the center point, then use a T-square and draw lines in a couple of directions to aid in positioning the cutter.

2. Set the cutter to 5" (12.7 cm) with a 2" (5.1 cm) differential.

3. Position the cutter on the center point on the matboard. Align the guide marks on the cutter with the pencil lines. Push the cutter down onto the matboard; little pins at the bottom of the cutter will hold it in place.

4. Insert the blade. Guide the blade as it curves around, cutting the opening.

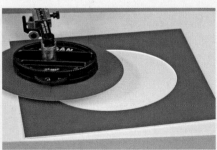

5. Complete the cut.

6. Finished oval mat

Cutting an Arched Mat

An arched mat is made with two mat openings, an oval or circle and a rectangle, overlapping one another. For visual balance, the top mat border is usually slightly smaller than the side and bottom borders to compensate for the large amount of matting visible around the arch.

With a true arched mat, the rectangle and curved openings meet precisely. Cut the oval first.

Oval opening = 5" × 7" (12.7 × 17.8 cm)
Rectangle opening = 5" × 7" (12.7 × 17.8 cm)

To cut the oval opening, it is necessary to find the center of the oval. The center of the width is easy—simply make a pencil mark at the middle

point of the horizontal measurement of the matboard; in this case it is 5" (12.7 cm).

To determine the distance from the top of the matboard to the center of the oval mat border, use the following calculation:

(2" [5.1 cm]) + half the height of the oval (½ of 7" [17.8 cm] = 3½" [8.9 cm])
2" + 3½" = 5½" (14 cm) [5.1 + 8.8 = 35.6 cm]

The point where the two lines intersect is where the oval cutter should be placed. The difference between the height and width of the opening is 2" (5.1 cm), so that is the differential setting on the oval cutter.

If there is any irregularity where the two openings meet at the sides of the mat, use an emery board to gently smooth the line.

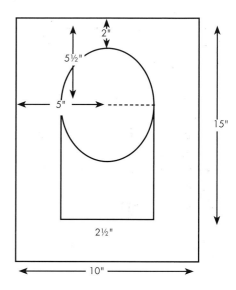

Cutting a Notched Arch Mat

When cutting an arched mat, it can be very difficult to cut the two openings so that they meet seamlessly. A notched arch, as shown here, is much simpler to make. The notches create an attractive additional angle. Cut the round opening first, then the rectangle.

Outside mat size = 13" × 15½" (33 × 39.4 cm)
Circle opening = 6½" (16.5 cm)
Rectangle opening = 8" × 9" (20.3 × 22.9 cm)

The center of the circle from the top of the mat is
2" (5.1 cm) + half of the height of the circle (3¼" [8.3 cm]) = 5¼" (13.3 cm)

The center of the circle from the side of the mat is
2½" (6.4 cm) + half the width of the circle (3¼" [8.3 cm]) = 5¾" (14.6 cm)

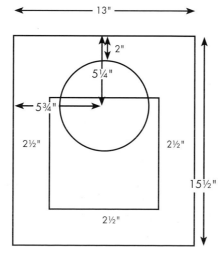

The point where the two lines intersect is where the oval cutter should be placed. With a circle, the difference between the height and width of the opening is 0", so 0 is the differential setting on the oval cutter.

MAT DECORATION

The Basics of Decoration

The surface of a mat can be decorated to enhance the visual presentation of the art. The goal is to add something that improves the presentation—the decoration should not overwhelm the art. As a general rule of proportion, the decoration should be within the first one-third of matting from the opening. For decorative lines surrounding the mat opening, it is best to vary the width of the decorative elements.

Decorative accent lines surrounding the mat opening can enhance the presentation of artwork. Light ink lines and a subtle wash of color decorate the mat on this pastoral English landscape.

Making a Fabric-Covered Mat

A typical matboard has a paper surface. Covering a mat with fabric adds richness and texture that can be elegant, sophisticated, formal, or even earthy, depending on the fabric. Most any medium-weight, even-weave fabric can be used to cover a mat, from velvet to linen. Other textiles, such as leather or vinyl, may work as well. When covering a matboard with fabric, it is generally best to use a light cream, gray, or beige board, as bright white or dark matboards can show through and affect the appearance of the fabric. Notice that the mat is cut before being covered with fabric; this is because most fabrics fray or wrinkle along the mat opening if cut after mounting. A reverse-bevel mat makes it easier to shape the fabric at the corners.

Method 1: Using an Adhesive-covered Board

To attach the fabric to the board, use a sheet of double-sided adhesive, or purchase an adhesive-coated board like the one used in this example.

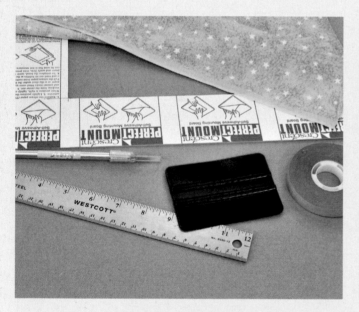

1. Cut the board to the size of the mat. Cut a piece of fabric the same size or, to create some "wiggle-room," cut the fabric a little larger than the mat, and trim it to size after step 4. Place the board in the mat cutter face up to make a reverse bevel. Cut the mat. Remove the fallout

2. Remove the paper cover from the adhesive. Carefully position the fabric on the right side of the board, aligning the weave of the fabric with the edge of the board.

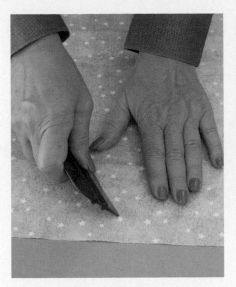

3. Use a burnisher or squeegee to adhere the fabric to the surface of the board.

4. Place the fabric-covered board face down on the worktable, and cut the fabric in the window with a sharp craft blade. Make a diagonal slice toward each corner, being careful to stop just a bit short of the corner.

5. Where the diagonal cuts end, cut out and remove the rectangle of fabric from the center of the window.

6. Place strips of double-sided tape surrounding the mat opening, about ½" (1.3 cm) from the opening.

7. Guide the flaps of fabric around the edges of the mat opening, and adhere them to the back of the mat.

8. Smooth the fabric at the corners, easing it around the edges. The mat is completed.

Method 2: Wet Mounting

Use a liquid adhesive such as white fabric or craft glue. Spray adhesive is not recommended—it does not hold securely over time, and it can stain the fabric. To prepare for mounting: Cut a piece of fabric to size; it is usually best to cut the fabric bigger than needed, trimming it to size after mounting. Cut a piece of matboard to size. Cut the mat face up to make a reverse bevel.

1. Using a flat brush, apply glue evenly to the surface of the mat. Thin the glue with a little water if necessary—not too much water or the adhesive will soak into the board.

2. Working quickly, while the adhesive is wet, position the fabric carefully on the mat, aligning the weave of the fabric with the straight edges of the board.

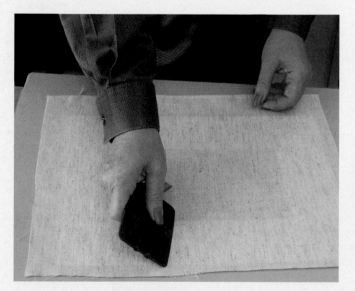

3. Use a burnisher or squeegee to adhere the fabric to the surface of the board. Don't use too much pressure, or the glue will be pushed away from some areas. Allow the adhesive to dry.

4. Place the mat face down on the worktable. Using a sharp craft blade, make a diagonal slice about 1" (2.5 cm) long at each corner, being careful to stop just a bit short of the corner. Where the diagonal cuts end, slice and remove the rectangle of fabric from the center of the window.

5. Trim the excess fabric from the edges of the board.

6. Place strips of double-sided tape surrounding the mat opening, about ¼" (6 mm) from the opening.

7. Guide the flaps of fabric around the edges of the mat opening, and adhere them to the back of the mat.

8. The mat is completed.

Making a Paper-Covered Mat

Paper can be mounted to a mat using the same process shown for making a fabric-wrapped mat. There is a wealth of beautiful papers available for crafting–especially scrapbooking papers. Any 8" × 10" (20.3 × 25.4 cm) mat can be covered with a single sheet of this paper; larger mats such as 11" × 14" (27.9 × 35.6 cm) will have to be pieced or can be covered with wrapping paper or other large paper. To burnish the paper to the matboard, roll a brayer, swipe a squeegee, or stroke lightly with a scrap of matboard. Be sure the paper is not too thin or it will wrinkle and tear; this is more of a problem if using wet paste rather than sheets of double-sided adhesive. If the texture of wrinkled paper sounds interesting, try using torn pieces of tissue paper, encouraging small wrinkles rather than smoothing the paper onto the mat.

With pattern and color, a paper-covered mat can "set the mood" for the framing design. Here paper is being applied to a sheet of adhesive-covered board. The mat may be cut after the paper is mounted to the board, eliminating the need to wrap the paper around the opening of a mat.

Deep Bevel Mats

Use foam center board and a standard bevel (not reverse) to make a deep-bevel paper-covered mat. Deep-bevel mats have a distinctive character that looks good on most types of art. To avoid problems with the paper separating at the corner, wrap each side of the mat separately, or decorate the corners with a small strip of matching or contrasting paper.

Embellished Mats

Because the surface of a matboard is essentially a sheet of paper, many stickers, rubber stamps, and other embellishments for scrapbooking and card-making are suitable for decorating mats. Better yet, many of the products are already coated with adhesive for easy application; if not, use tiny dots of white glue or double-sided adhesive. The look can be elegant (a monogram in one corner of the mat), playful (cartoon characters sprinkled all over the mat), romantic (vining flowers surrounding the mat opening), or many other styles.

Dimensional embellishments are also an option: beads, seashells, and other small items can be glued to a mat. If the frame will have glazing in it, there will need to be space in the frame for the embellishment, as when making a shadow box. Note: Some embellishments may be attached to fabric-covered mats with fabric glue, but test first to make sure the glue holds.

A simple embellishment can be created with a few round holes (made with a hole punch) and a length of ¼" (6 mm) ribbon.

To commemorate a special celebration, have guests autograph a mat at the party; then use the mat to frame the announcement or invitation.

French Matting

This traditional mat decoration method uses ink lines and pale washes of watercolor to surround the opening of the mat. French matting usually seems dignified or elegant depending on the colors and configuration of lines and washes. Traditionally used to frame engravings, hand-colored prints, and watercolor paintings, French matting has become a popular decoration for art prints, photo portraits, and important documents as well. The matboard color is usually white, cream, or a very light pastel.

Purists use an old-fashioned ruling pen and permanent ink to draw the lines, but any fine-tip, permanent felt-tip marker that does not bleed into the mat will be fine (try fine-tip pigmented pens). Good quality colored pencils may also be used. Use a cork-backed ruler to guide the pen or pencil.

The wash panel can be made with any student-grade tube of liquid watercolor or the bottled acrylic paints sold in the craft stores in dozens of colors. (If using a traditional ruling pen to draw lines on the mat, the craft acrylic paint can be used full strength in place of ink.) The wash of color in the panel is supposed to be very pale and transparent, so it is mostly water with just a dab of paint. The brush should be a ½" (1.3 cm)-wide flat soft brush; the acrylic-bristle type sold in craft stores is fine.

Drawing the Lines with a Fine Marker

1. With a pencil and ruler, make dots (actually small circles, so as not to make dents in the mat) near the corners of the mat, ¼" (6 mm) from the mat opening. Draw lines at the intersections of the four corners to indicate where to start and stop each ink line. Make a second set of pencil dots and lines ¾" (1.9 cm) away from the mat opening.

2. Line up the ruler along one of the inner sets of dots. Draw a line with the marker from one corner dot to another, being careful not to let the marker linger at any point or overlap in the corners.

3. Turn the mat, and line up the ruler with a second set of inner dots. Draw a line. Continue around the mat.

4. Draw the second set of lines using the outer set of dots. Erase all pencil marks.

Ink lines can be used alone, without a panel of color, for a simple accent on mats.

Making a Watercolor Wash Panel

1. Mix a pale wash of color. Test on a scrap of the same color of matboard to test the color.

2. With clean water, use the brush to apply a light wash to the panel between the ink lines. This helps the color to absorb evenly.

3. Dip the brush into the watercolor wash. It should be wet but not dripping. Starting 1" (2.5 cm) away from any corner, rest the tip of the brush lightly on the matboard, and begin to pull the brush along the panel. Add more wash color to the brush as needed, and begin slightly before the end of the last brushstroke each time the brush is set onto the mat.

4. Near the area where the end of the wash panel will connect with the dry paint at the beginning, lift the brush and dab it on a paper towel to remove excess wash. Use the brush to blend the start and finish of the wash.

Colored Bevels

A colored bevel is a simple but effective mat decoration. Bevels can be colored with acrylic craft paint or colored pencils. Cut the mat first, and then surround the opening with removable pressure-sensitive tape to protect the surface of the mat. Note: Felt-tip markers can be used, but test them on a scrap board to make sure the ink does not bleed onto the surface of the mat.

The purple bevel provides a thin but vivid accent line that coordinates with the color of this engraving.

Window Accents for Mats

We have seen how a double mat creates an attractive accent line within a mat window. Other materials can also be used to make a decorative inner border.

Sometimes a narrow wood or plastic moulding called "fillet moulding" is used to create this accent line. Fillet moulding is made expressly for this purpose, with a narrow rabbet that attaches to the back of the mat, and a decorative lip that is exposed. It is cut with a beveled corner just like regular moulding. The decorative lip may be a simple scoop or half-round design, or it may have a line of small beads or an embossed pattern. Common colors are gold, silver, stained wood tones, or black. The mat for a fillet is usually cut with a reverse bevel, shown in Cutting Mats (page 77). Glue or double-sided tape may be used to attach the fillet to the back of the mat.

Begin by attaching one piece of fillet securely in the mat opening. Then attach an adjacent piece, matching the corners. Continue around the mat opening.

Paper strips, cut about 1" (2.5 cm) wide and folded in half, allow framers to use everything from wrapping paper to wallpaper to make an accent liner. As long as the material is thin and will lay flat in the frame, it has potential. This is a decorative framing technique, but it can be used with valuable artwork if it can be determined that the liner material has the qualities necessary for conservation framing. Use Magic Mending Tape to attach the liner material to the back of the matboard.

Lace adds a pretty, feminine, or romantic feeling. Use Magic Mending Tape to attach the lace to the back of the mat.

A fillet should fit flush against the mat opening, with well-matched corners. The fillet creates a ridge on the back of the mat. Use matboard strips attached with double-sided tape to build up the mat until it is level with the fillet—this must be done or the tilt in the matboard will weaken the attachment of the fillet and cause buckling of the mat.

BUILDING PICTURE FRAMES

Joining a Frame

Building frames is called "joining" in the picture framing industry. There are several methods for joining frames, depending on the frame material and the equipment available. Most frames require four straight pieces of moulding cut with a 45-degree miter at each end. Each piece of cut moulding is called a "rail."

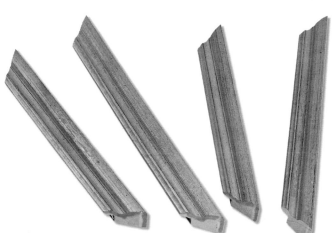

Four pieces of moulding with mitred corners are needed to make a typical picture frame. There are several methods for joining the pieces together.

Assembling Sectional Frames

Sectional frames are precut rails of moulding with mitered ends. They are sold in pairs, and each frame requires two pairs, one for the length of the frame and one for the width. The corners are joined by the DIY framer using the hardware designed for the frame. The most common type of sectional frame is metal (normally aluminum), but wood sectional frames are also available. There are many sizes and profiles, but the assembly methods are similar. If ordering a sectional frame, make sure the joining hardware is included; sometimes it must be ordered separately.

Assembling a Wood Sectional Frame

The corner of each rail has a slot routed out to hold a plastic wedge that will join the frame.

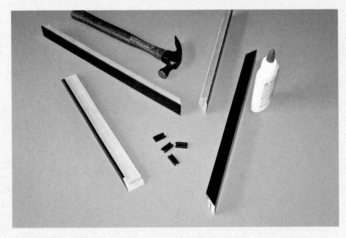

1. Lay the four rails of the frame face down with corners matched.

2. Squirt a little bit of wood glue onto one end of raw moulding on one rail of the frame. Place the adjacent rail of the frame against the glued end.

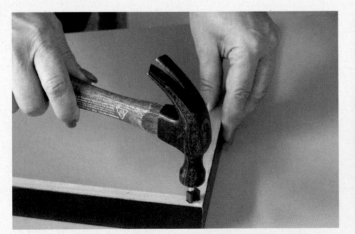

3. Holding the corner together, insert the joining wedges (these may be called thumbnails, dovetails, or angle pins) into the slot in the corner. Tap with a hammer if necessary.

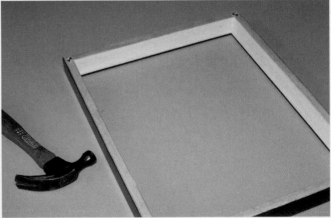

4. Repeat on the remaining three corners.

Assembling a Metal Sectional Frame

Fitting is the term framers use to describe the process of finishing the framing: securing the framing materials in the frame, sealing it up, and adding finishing touches like hangers and bumper pads. With a metal frame, building the frame and fitting are blended, so most of the process is covered in Fitting (page 111).

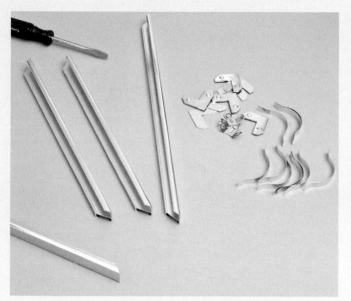

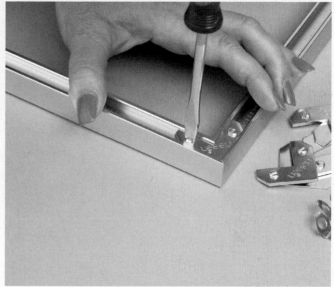

1. Four rails of metal moulding and a set of corner hardware are needed to join a metal frame. The hardware varies slightly depending on the manufacturer of the frame. Place the four rails and the hardware on the worktable.

2. Insert the corner hardware into the channel of one frame rail. Slide the adjoining rail onto the hardware, and tighten the screws with a screwdriver. Repeat to attach the third rail, then see Basic Fitting Procedure for Metal Frames (page 116).

Assembling a Clip Frame

Clip frames use simple clip hardware to hold the framing materials together. They are not really frames, because they do not fully surround the framing materials, so the edges of the glazing and other framing materials are exposed. There are two main types: those that allow a variable size, and those that include a backing board that determines the size. Clip frames either snap over the framing materials, or use a cord to join the clip hardware behind the backing board.

Variable-size clip frames, such as the Eubank Frame, use a string or wire to secure a set of clips and can adapt to a range of sizes. This type of frame can usually accommodate at least one mat. The metal clips are visible as small silver bars on the face of the picture.

Custom-Cut Frames

A wide variety of custom-cut wood and metal mouldings is available from mail order and Internet sources. In professional framing, a frame that is ordered precut is called "chopped." A chopped frame is four pieces (rails) of moulding cut to a specific size by a supplier. DIY suppliers may call them "precut" or "custom cut" frames. Custom metal frames are assembled using the same sort of hardware used for precut metal sectional frames; check to see if hardware is included in the frame order, because sometimes it must be ordered separately. Unassembled custom wood frames usually have routed corners and corner wedges for assembly, but they may simply be miter-cut rails of moulding that need to be nailed together. Check to see what is available from each supplier. Ask about the "allowance policy" when ordering any custom-cut frame: ⅛" (3 mm) is customary, but some may use 1/16" (2 mm) or cut the frame exactly as ordered.

This is a custom-size "chopped" frame ready to be assembled.

DIY Frame-Making

For some people, cutting and building their own frames is an essential part of do-it-yourself framing. This is a carpentry project, using saws, vises, and other woodworking equipment. As always in framing, accurate measuring and cutting are essential for success. Problem-solving abilities come in handy: Warped moulding and fragile moulding finishes are a couple of the typical challenges encountered when making frames.

Sources for Picture Frame Moulding

Moulding for picture frames is sold in sticks of varying lengths. The most common are 8' (2.4 m) and 10' (3 m), but there are others, such as 6' (1.8 m) and 12' (3.7 m). Local lumberyards or home improvement stores may carry some picture frame moulding, although most of the moulding available from these sources is decorative moulding, with no rabbet to hold framing materials. Online sources tend to offer a bigger selection. The sticks should be as straight as possible-—warped moulding creates serious problems when cutting and joining frame corners.

The vast majority of the thousands of available picture frame mouldings are sold to wholesale buyers only. There

are many wholesale framing supply distributors; if there is one in your area, find out about their terms. If you have a vendor's license, you may be able to set up an account. Some distributors also sell to artists and may sell to DIY framers as well. There is probably a minimum order, but it may be reasonably low.

When buying moulding to cut with a saw, consider the type of wood. Many picture frame mouldings are made from woods that are easily cut, without chipping the finish. But some are hard, dense woods, such as oak or maple, and some ornate frames have a fragile finish. Find out all you can about a moulding before buying it to make sure it is something your equipment can handle.

Measuring Moulding

Once the framing is designed, it is time to determine how much moulding will be needed for the frame. At this point, the length and width of the frame opening is known, and two pieces of moulding will be needed for each dimension; but that only accounts for the "running inches"—the number of inches (centimeters) it takes to go around the opening of the frame. Additional moulding is needed to extend to the outer edges of the mitered corners. Each of the four sides of the frame will have a 45-degree miter cut at each end, and every one of those eight cuts requires an extra moulding width of moulding to accommodate the corners. To determine the moulding width, measure across the top of the moulding, including the rabbet. Then multiply that number by 8 to determine the amount of additional moulding needed. For example, if the moulding is 2" (5.1 cm) wide, the frame will need 2" (5.1 cm) × 8 cuts, or 16" (40.6 cm) of additional moulding.

Note: Strictly speaking, because the frame should be cut with an allowance of ⅛" (3 mm) in each direction, an additional ¼" (6 mm) of moulding is needed, but this small fraction is not used in the moulding calculation for individual frames. When buying a moulding to make a dozen or more frames, it may be important to consider those few extra inches (centimeters).

In addition to the running inches, an extra "moulding width" of moulding is needed for each of the eight miter cuts to allow for the distance from the rabbet to the outer corners. Measure across the face of the moulding and multiply by 8. The running inches total plus the moulding width total gives you the amount of moulding needed to build the frame. In this example, the frame is 16" × 20" and the moulding is 2" (5.1 cm) wide. 72" + (8 × 1½") = 72" + 12" = 84" [183 + (8 × 3.8) = 213.4 cm] of moulding, or 7' (2.1 m) of moulding.

This example determines the amount of 1½" (3.8 cm)-wide moulding needed for a 16" × 20" (40.6 × 50.8 cm) frame. Two times the length of the framing materials, plus two times the width of the materials, equals the number of running inches (centimeters) of moulding needed to go around the materials at the rabbet measurement. (16 × 2) + (20 × 2) = 32 + 40 = 72 running inches. The extra moulding needed for the miter cuts will be added to this amount.

Moulding Length

If long sticks of moulding must be cut for easier shipping, be sure the resulting lengths will yield the frames you want! For example, a 10' (3 m) stick of moulding may be cut into two 5' (1.5 m) sticks, or one 6' (1.8 m) and one 4' (1.2 m). This can make a difference, depending on the dimensions of the frames being built.

Cutting Wood Moulding

For DIY framing (and for many professionals as well), picture frame moulding is cut with a saw. A clean, accurate 45-degree miter cut is essential. A limited range of mouldings can be cut with a hand saw and miter box, and this is all some DIY framers ever need. A manual miter saw made for cutting moulding is a more practical and versatile option for framers who will cut moulding frequently.

Professional framers use an electric miter saw, which can cut almost any wood picture frame moulding. For the DIY framer who already owns such a saw or wants to invest in this level of equipment, note that there are different types of blades (carbide or steel, varying number of teeth, and so on), each with its own advantages. Read the information from a couple of different manufacturers to determine the best blade for your use. Professional framers prefer a blade with many small teeth, not a rip saw. Many framers prefer a 10" or 12" (25.5 or 30.5 cm), 80-tooth, carbide blade with alternately beveled teeth, which will cut all but the widest and deepest of mouldings. A saw fence with a 45-degree angled scale is crucial for consistent, accurate cutting.

Regardless of the type of equipment, use safety precautions when cutting moulding: Eye masks protect against flying wood chips; hand guards on saws protect fingers from the saw blade. Also control the sawdust the operator might breathe.

There are several reasons why a miter cut may not be smooth, such as a dull saw blade or damp wood. Rough cuts should be sanded before attempting to assemble the frame. There are sanding tools sold specifically for this purpose, but unless you need it for a large number of frames, an ordinary sanding block is suitable. The best type of sandpaper depends on the type of wood and roughness of the cut. Sanding can also be used to make mitered corners align correctly. After cutting four pieces of moulding for a frame, lay the pieces in their proper position on a flat table and examine the alignment of the miters at each corner. Sand the miter cuts if needed to create well-matched corners, but go slow—make small adjustments and test again.

Use sandpaper to smooth rough cuts and make small adjustments, to create well-matched corners before building the frame. A medium grit works on most types of wood.

This is a basic miter box and saw. Pairs of slots in the box guide the saw to cut the moulding at the desired angle.

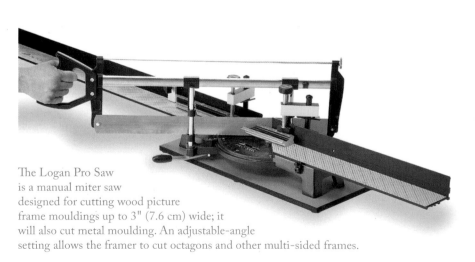

The Logan Pro Saw is a manual miter saw designed for cutting wood picture frame mouldings up to 3" (7.6 cm) wide; it will also cut metal moulding. An adjustable-angle setting allows the framer to cut octagons and other multi-sided frames.

Square and rectangular frames are cut with a 45-degree miter. Hexagon and other multi-sided frames require other angles. Some saws offer angle adjustments, or a jig may be used to create the correct angle.

Methods for Joining Wood Frames

There are several ways for the DIY framer to join wood frames. Regardless of the method chosen for joining miter-cut wood frame moulding, the corners should first be glued together, using a glue made for wood. This can be done corner-by-corner using a corner vise, or all four corners at once using a strap clamp. There are some super-hold glues that claim they will never break down, but glue alone is not sufficient (no matter what kind) except on very small frames. Wood changes as it ages, drying and shrinking; any glue will eventually fail.

The most basic joining method uses a corner vise or corner clamps and a hammer and nails. This is a strong, reliable way to join frames. The appropriate nails are straight, small-headed wire nails, also called brads, which are available in a variety of sizes. Choose the size according to the hardness of the wood and the size of the frame. A tack hammer is a good tool for inserting the brads. It may be necessary to first drill in very hard wood such as oak or ash. To avoid marking the moulding as the hammer reaches the frame surface, push the brad through a small square of matboard before beginning to insert the brad. When the matboard rests against the frame, pull it off of the brad. Use a nail set to finish sinking the brad, and sink it about ⅛" (3 mm) beneath the surface of the frame.

A strap clamp (also called a band clamp) consists of a long strap that wraps around the outer perimeter of an unjoined frame as it lays on a flat surface, and a clamp that can be locked when the frame corners are perfectly aligned. This can be used to align a wood sectional frame before joining, or to securely hold a frame while glue is drying.

The narrow head, small tip, and balanced weight of a tack hammer make it a good choice for building picture frames.

A small amount of wood glue is applied to two mitered ends of moulding; then they are placed in the corner vise and adjusted until they meet properly. The vise is tightened to firmly hold the moulding in place during the nailing process.

This is a typical corner vise used to join picture frames.

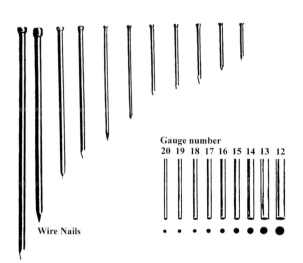

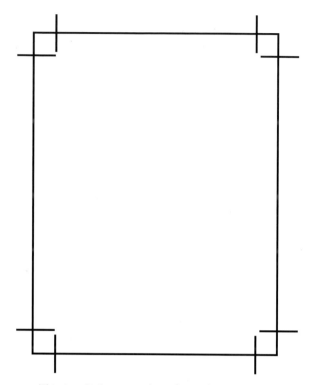

Brads come in different lengths and thicknesses to suit different mouldings.

This is called cross-nailing. Some framers believe this provides necessary strength; others think this makes unattractive and unnecessary holes.

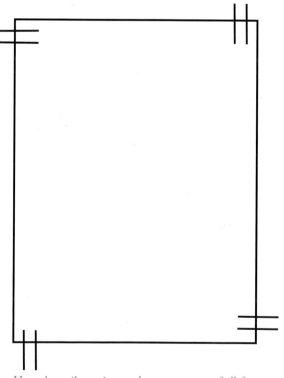

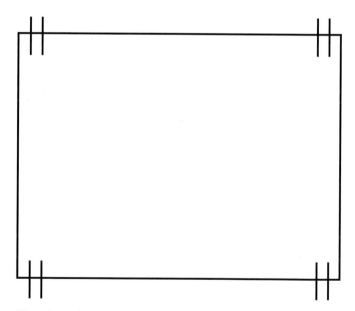

Here the nails are inserted at one corner of all four sides. This is a common method.

Here the nails are located in the top and bottom only, so nail holes are not seen when the frame is hanging.

The "hammer and nails" joining method creates visible nail holes that must be filled for a professional finish. Use a color-coordinated filler made for wood. Non-drying nail filler in many colors, made especially for filling nail holes in frames, are available from some framing suppliers through their Web sites.

Another traditional joining method employs wood disks called biscuits that fit into slots routed in the corners of the frame. Some woodworkers consider this "no nail" method superior to all others, and it is a very nice way to join frames at home for those experienced with this technique—but it is rarely used by professional framers.

Professional framers like to join frames with a V-nailer, a machine that inserts V-shaped hardware into the underside of the moulding, so there are no nail holes in the frame finish. Two rails of moulding are placed in the machine with the miters aligned, a lever is pressed, and the hardware is released. Small versions of the V-nailer, capable of joining many types of wood moulding, are available for the DIY framer.

The Logan Studio Joiner is a V-nailer made for DIY framing. It can be used to join mouldings up to 2½" (6.4 cm) wide. The moulding goes into the machine face down, and the V-shaped nails are inserted one at a time. As usual, glue should be applied to the miter cuts before joining.

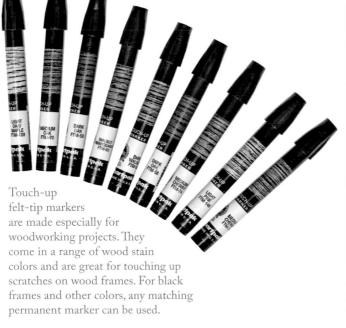

Touch-up felt-tip markers are made especially for woodworking projects. They come in a range of wood stain colors and are great for touching up scratches on wood frames. For black frames and other colors, any matching permanent marker can be used.

Nail holes should be filled for an attractive join. Simply push some matching color filler into the holes, and wipe the excess away with a dry cloth or paper towel.

FITTING:
FINISHING THE FRAMING

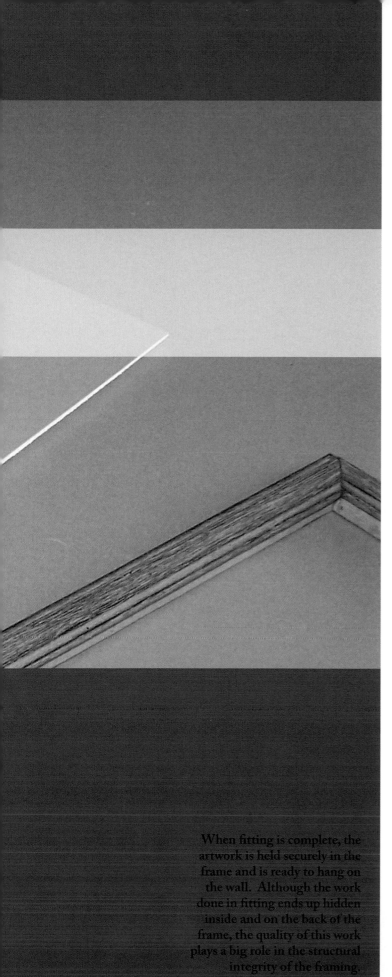

The Process of Fitting

The process of finishing the framing (installing all of the materials in the frame, sealing it up, and adding hanging hardware) is called fitting. There are several techniques, depending on the type of framing and the preference of the framer. The first step in fitting is gathering all of the materials that will go into a frame and stacking them in order. The fitting materials referred to in this chapter are discussed in The Tools of the Trade (page 42).

When fitting is complete, the artwork is held securely in the frame and is ready to hang on the wall. Although the work done in fitting ends up hidden inside and on the back of the frame, the quality of this work plays a big role in the structural integrity of the framing.

The Sandwich Fit

Tiny bits of debris often find their way into the stack of materials that go into a frame. This is a common source of frustration for framers, who have to reopen a completed framing to chase a small but obvious piece of debris.

For any framing that includes glazing, the sandwich fit is an extremely helpful technique for keeping materials clean and dust-free during fitting. It also serves as a moisture barrier for art that will hang in damp areas such as bathrooms and basements. By surrounding the framing materials with a U-channel of tape, the sandwich fit allows framers to prepare a "one-time" fit.

1. Thoroughly clean the glazing on the side that will face the art. The side that will face outward will be cleaned at the very end of fitting.

2. Brush all dust and lint from the matting. Assemble the framing materials face up in this order: backing board with art attached, mats, glazing.

3. Using ¾" (1.9 cm) Magic Mending Tape, run a line of tape along the edge of the glass on one side, allowing just ⅛" (3 mm) of the tape to rest on the surface of the glass. Be very careful to prevent bare fingers from brushing the sharp edge of the glass. Break the tape when you reach the corner.

4. Wrap the remainder of the tape around the edge of the framing materials. Secure the tape to the back of the backing board. Do not pull hard on the tape—the wrap should be close, but not tight.

5. Finish the remaining three sides in the same manner.

Filler Board

Except in small frames, such as 5" × 7" (12.7 × 17.8 cm), the backing board behind the art generally needs additional support so it does not buckle or bow over the years. If the art is attached to (or fully mounted to) a foam center board, this may be sufficient support, unless the frame is larger than 24" × 30" (61 × 76.2 cm). Otherwise, additional sheets of board, called filler board, should be added. The rabbet of the frame does not need to be filled; one sheet of filler board is usually sufficient. Matboard, mounting board, and foam center board are all suitable for filler board.

Sealing Wood Frames

If acids are bad for most kinds of art, won't the acidic raw wood interior of a frame be harmful? Some professional framers and museum conservators say yes; others say no. To be on the safe side when framing very valuable artwork, do what the professionals do—seal the inner surface of the frame. There is Frame Sealing Tape (from Lineco) made especially for this purpose, or you can use long strips of Magic Mending Tape, or coat the wood with clear liquid acrylic medium and allow it to thoroughly dry.

Dust Cover Paper

Professional framers complete the fit with a dust cover, which is a sheet of paper that completely covers the back of the frame. The paper keeps dust and debris out of the framing and creates a "finished" look. Some framers use ordinary brown kraft paper, some use black kraft paper for a more sophisticated look, and some use a blue-gray conservation paper made especially for framing. DIY framers sometimes use brown paper bags or pretty wrapping paper. White glue or double-sided tape is used to adhere the paper to the back of the frame. Some framers worry about using acidic papers for a dust cover, but many consider the risk so small that they use the special conservation paper only on very valuable art.

Choosing the Hanging Hardware

Wall Buddies
are strong and make it easy to hang large frames level.

The hardware discussed here is for framed art. There are adhesive-backed linen and other types of hangers for art mounted with no frame, such as a poster attached to foam center board, but these hangers are not strong enough for framed pieces. Here is a general guideline for choosing appropriate hanging hardware, although decisions about each frame project must be determined according to the weight and structure of the project.

- For small to medium frames: A sawtooth hanger or small screw eyes and light wire

- For medium to large frames: Strong screw eyes with strong wire, or D-rings (strap hangers) with or without strong wire

- For large or heavy frames: Heavy-duty D-rings (strap hangers) with no wire, or WallBuddies (a self-leveling hanger)

Security hangers are made mostly for public spaces. There are several types available, but they typically work with a two-part system in which a part on the frame locks into a part on the wall. They are good for keeping framed art from being dislodged in rambunctious areas, but they will not stop a determined thief, willing to damage the wall to remove the frame.

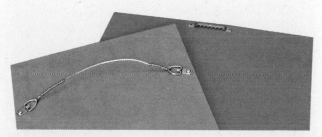

The appropriate hardware depends on the size and weight of the frame.

Basic Fitting Procedure for Wood Frames

1. Thoroughly clean the glazing on the side that will face the art. (The side that will face outward will be cleaned at the very end of the fitting.)

2. Brush all dust and lint from the matting and art.

3. Assemble the framing materials face up in this order: backing board with art attached, mats, glazing. If using the sandwich fit, tape this unit together.

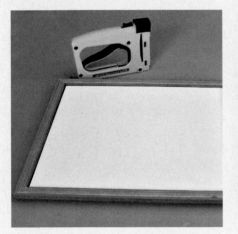

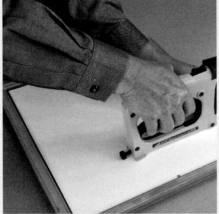

4. Place the frame face down on a clean work surface. Insert the framing material into the frame. Add filler board.

5. Secure the materials in the frame. Brads may be tapped into the rabbet of the frame with a small hammer, or a nail driver (or point driver) may be used. Do not press down on the framing materials. Too much pressure can cause materials to buckle over time. Rest the brads on the surface of the filler board and tap them straight into the wood, or rest the point driver on the filler board and shoot the point straight, not downward at an angle.

6. Attach a dust cover using glue or double-sided tape. Use an oversized piece of paper, and then trim the excess with a sharp blade. Sometimes amateurs staple a sheet of matboard to the back of the frame, but the edge of the matboard is visible when the framing is hung on a wall.

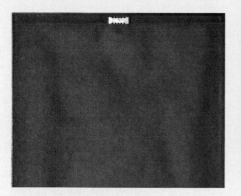

7. Attach the hanging hardware.

Sawtooth hanger (for small frames only): Match the center of the top rail of the frame to the center of the hanger. Attach the hanger with small nails or simply tap the hanger into the frame, depending on the style of hanger.

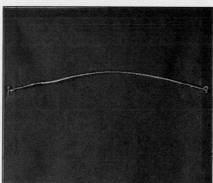

Screw eyes and wire: Measure and mark each side rail of the frame about one-fourth of the way from the top of the frame. Make a small hole with an awl. Insert a screw eye into each hole, and twist to install. If using braided wire, insert wire into one screw eye, passing several inches of wire through the eye. Wrap the end of the wire around the screw eye and pass it through the eye a second time. Wrap the excess wire neatly around the main wire to secure it. Extend the wire across the back of the frame through the screw eye twice, leaving a little but not a lot of slack in the wire. Secure the end of the wire.

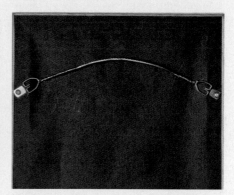

D-rings and wire: The D-rings should be installed at an angle, tilted toward one another, to create a more natural tension for the wire. Install the wire as described in the previous step for screw eyes.

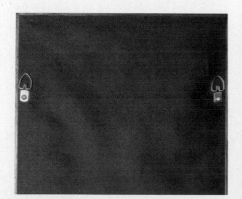

D-rings alone (strong support for large or heavy frames): Screw the D-rings in place. Do not attach wire to the D-rings: Each ring is meant to hang over a separate hook on the wall; this gives the frame strong support and does not overstress the hardware.

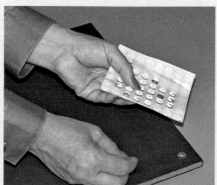

8. This step is optional but recommended: Add bumper pads to the bottom corners of the frame, They cushion the wall from marks made by the frame, allow air circulation behind the frame, and hold the frame straight on the wall, compensating for the bump created by the hanging hardware.

9. Clean the face of the glazing with glass cleaner and a soft cloth.

Extra Support for Large Wood Frames

Very large or heavy framing projects may require additional bracing across the back of the frame, horizontally, vertically, or in both directions. The purpose of bracing is to support the four rails of the frame, to prevent the sides from bowing outward and the lower corners from separating at the miters. This is advanced framing, requiring decisions about the engineering of the frame, as well as the location and materials of the bracing that would be best for the project. Those with carpentry skills can probably create what is needed, but others should consult a professional framer. Remember that any frame that needs bracing will need strong hangers in the wall as well.

Basic Fitting Procedure for Metal Frames

These instructions will apply to most sectional metal frames. There are a few variations. One style of metal frame is deep and has two channels for two sets of hardware, one at the front of the frame and the other at the back, for extra strength. A few metal frames are manufactured with a channel that holds "press-in" plastic hardware to join the corners.

1. Lay the four rails of metal face down on a clean worktable (the surface of a metal frame is easily scratched). Insert corner hardware into one end of one rail. Slide the adjoining rail onto the corner hardware. Adjust for good alignment, then tighten the screws on the corner hardware. Repeat on the opposite end of the first rail. The frame is now a three-sided unit.

2. Stack the glazing (cleaned on the side facing the artwork), mats, artwork, and backing board. Tape them together using the sandwich fit if desired. Place the stack face down. If the backing board is only a matboard, add another matboard or foam center board to the stack as filler board.

3. Slide the stack of materials into the framing channel of the frame.

4. The excess space in the framing channel must be filled to hold the glazing to the front of the frame. This may be done in two ways:

a) The channel may be filled completely with matboard or other board. Simply cut boards to the size of the other framing materials, and slip them into the channel until the channel is full but not tight. Paper dust covers are not used with metal frames, so this board serves as the backing.

b) Curved metal "spring clips," which are typically included with the metal frame hardware, may be inserted into the excess space along the edges of the frame. This is done after the fourth rail of moulding has been attached. See step 6.

5. Insert corner hardware into the fourth rail of moulding, and slide the hardware into the hardware channel. Tighten the screws.

 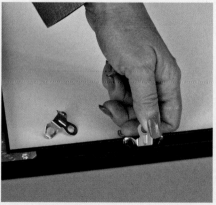 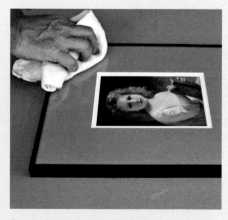

6. If using spring clips, lay them on the back of the framing materials, spaced evenly against the edges of the frame, positioned like little hills. Compress each clip and slide it under the lip of the frame channel, pushing it as far as it will go. A screwdriver is helpful for this. Beware of flying spring clips, which can get away from a framer and fling themselves hard and fast in any direction!

7. Install the hanging hardware. This may be a sawtooth hanger, which snaps into the hardware channel at the top of the frame, or two pieces of hardware with holes for stringing wire, which snap into the side channels. (Note: One type of hardware slips into the side channels of the frame before the fourth rail is attached; this hardware should be inserted before step 5.)

8. Clean the face of the glass.

Using Spacers in a Frame

For framing that will last a long time in good condition, glazing should not be placed directly against art; mats are the most common solution. When there is no matting, spacers may be used to separate the glazing from the art. Econospace and Innerspace are two brand names of small rectangular tubes with an adhesive backing that fit in the rabbet of the frame between the glazing and the art. Spacers can also be made using narrow strips of matboard that run around the entire perimeter of the frame interior; use one or two layers and attach them to the edges of the glazing, hidden in the rabbet, with double-sided tape. Note: Although spacers solve one problem, they can create another: large or thin art on paper may slump or bow into the airspace between the glazing and the art. Full mounting is the only sure way to prevent this.

Illustration of hollow, rectangular Econospace in a frame

Installing an Easel Back

An easel back allows the frame to stand rather than hang on a wall. This is normally used on photos and other small artwork, usually no bigger than 11" x 14" (27.9 x 35.6 cm) frames. Larger frames with easel backs are too heavy, and the easel back weakens and splays out, tilting the frame backward. Photo frames come supplied with easel backs, but they can be purchased in small standard sizes from framing suppliers for use with custom frames.

For a wood frame that you want to reopen from time to time, purchase the size that fits the opening of the frame and attach it to the frame with turn buttons at intervals of about 3" or 4" (7–10 cm); for a permanent fit, use small nails. For a metal frame, simply use the easel back as the final backing board, inserting it into the metal frame before attaching the fourth rail of the frame.

Trim the easel back to the outer size of the frame, then use small nails to attach it to the back of the frame.

A Note about Framing Art Between Two Pieces of Glazing

This is a decorator-inspired style: The art is pressed between two pieces of glazing, so the art appears to be floating in the middle of the frame, and the wall color or wallpaper pattern shows through the glazing as a border for the art. The pressure of the two sheets of glazing alone will not hold the art in place over time—plus it is unhealthy for the art, as wrinkles often develop.

It is best to use spacers between the two sheets of glazing, hidden in the rabbet of the frame; use EconoSpace or narrow strips of matboard. Thoroughly clean the face of the back glazing to remove any adhesive-resistant residue. Attach decorative art to the back sheet of glazing with permanent double-sided tape. For valuable art, cut a piece of conservation matboard about ½" (1.3 cm) smaller than the art, float the art on the matboard using float hinges (page 136), then attach the matboard to the back sheet of the glazing with double-sided tape or self-adhesive corner pockets. Clean the top sheet of glazing and place it in the frame. Install the spacers. Add the art, attached to the back glazing. Use short brads or glazier's points to fit the materials in a wood frame, or the ends of the points will be visible in the framing.

This framing uses a special style of Framespace that provides two slots for glazing, one behind the art and the other in front of it, with space in between.

Fitting a Mirror

Follow the steps for fitting a wood or metal frame, but be very careful not to scratch the fragile coating on the back of the mirror. Also be sure to use a backing board to protect the mirror in the frame. Mirrors tend to be heavy, so it is important to use a strong frame and strong hanging hardware. Color the rabbet of the frame black to control the reflection of the rabbet in the mirror.

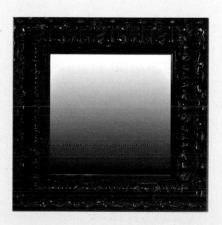

Fitting Art on Canvas

These tips apply to any paintings, photographs, needlepoint, or any other art that is stretched on stretcher bars or strainers.

Wood Frames

If the stretcher bars fit completely in the frame, use the typical fitting methods for wood frames. Most wood frames are not deep enough to comfortably hold art on canvas, so the canvas sticks out from the back of the frame. Offset clips are the most common type of hardware used for fitting a protruding canvas. A second option is canvas clips, which grip the frame rabbet and snap over standard stretcher bars. For DIY framing, "toenailing" (tapping long, thin nails at an angle from the edge of the stretcher bar into the frame) is another alternative. Whether using nails or clips, only a small number are needed, such as one on each side for an 11" x 14" (27.9 x 35.6 cm) frame, or three on each side for a 24" x 36" (61 x 91.4 cm) frame. A dust cover paper may be applied afterwards, covering the protruding stretcher bars and the clips or nail heads.

Offset clips provide a quick and easy method for fitting art on canvas. They are a good conservation method, because they hold the canvas by pressure alone; just four clips are sufficient for this painting. Note that the corners of the frame are resting on padded risers made by the framer. The risers keep the dimensional brushstrokes on the surface of the painting from touching the work table.

Many professional framers avoid toenailing, because the nails pierce the bars and sometimes pierce the sides of the canvas as well. However, toenailing is acceptable for decorative art on canvas. After inserting each nail, tap the head down onto the stretcher bar.

The points on one end of a canvas clip dig into the rabbet of the frame, while the other end snaps over the stretcher bar that holds the art. Be careful that the clips do not push against the canvas.

Metal Frames

Metal frames made especially for canvas have room for the canvas and a backing board. Sometimes there is additional room that should be filled with boards or spring clips.

Glazing and Spacers

Glazing is not typically used on paintings; however, if glazing is needed a spacer must be installed between the glazing and the art to keep the paint from sticking to the glazing and to preserve the dimensional texture of the paint. The spacer may be thin strips of matboard or strips of EconoSpace. The spacer is installed after the glazing is in place; then the painting is placed in the frame and fitted.

Liner moulding is used as a border when framing canvas. It can be used as a spacer by placing the glazing in the frame. Then place the assembled liner frame on top of the glazing and hold it in the frame with nails or framer's points (using a light touch to avoid breaking the glazing). Place the canvas in the rabbet of the liner and fit.

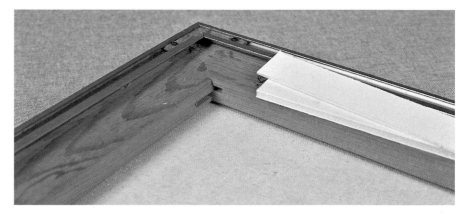

Long strips of foam center board may be pushed into the frame channel to fill the extra space, or spring clips may be used. Full sheets of matboard or foam center board are another option; they protect the back of the painting and create a nice finish.

A linen-covered liner is the classic border for art on canvas, and it also serves as a spacer when using glazing.

Floater Frames

These frames are made especially to show the edges of the canvas. The art is attached to the frame using screws that go through a ledge on the frame and into the back of the stretcher bars, so the canvas appears to float within the frame. Sticky-backed Velcro can also be used to hold the canvas to the frame.

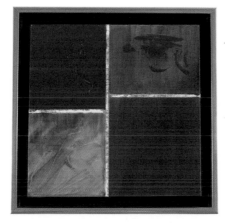

Strips of adhesive-backed hook and loop material (such as Velcro) were used to attach this canvas to the floater frame. One side of the material is pressed onto the back of the canvas, the other is pressed onto the ledge in the frame. Staples may be added for reinforcement.

Fitting Shadow Boxes

In many ways, the fitting process for shadow box frames is the same as for other types of art, but there is one significant difference: The interior sides of the frame will be visible, so they are part of the presentation of the items in the frame. Ready-made shadow box frames, and even some custom frames, come with finished interiors and a second rabbet (a back rabbet) to support the backing board (which holds the objects), but most custom shadow box frames will require the framer to do this interior finishing. There are two goals: Create an attractive finish for the inside of the frame, and create a ledge that serves as a back rabbet. Here are the two most common methods for accomplishing these goals.

Five-Piece Lining for Wood Frames

This is a simple, basic technique that lines the sides of the frame with strips of matboard. The four strips of matboard may be the same color as the backing board that contains the objects, or they may be a different color that coordinates with the other elements in the framing. The backing board is the fifth piece of the lining.

1. Lay the frame face down. Measure the depth of the frame—allowing for the thickness of the glazing, the backing board and the filler board. (One option is to place these materials in the frame and measure the remaining space.) Measure the width of one side of the frame interior.

2. Cut two strips of matboard to this size. Cut two strips of foam board to match the size of the matboard strips. Attach each strip of matboard to a strip of foam board with glue or double-sided tape.

3. Place the glazing in the frame. Apply glue plus a couple of short pieces of double-sided tape—to help the strips stay in place while the glue dries—to the two strips. Attach the strips to opposite sides of the frame, resting the bottom edges on the glazing.

4. Measure the remaining sides of the frame. Be precise, so the ends will match well. Cut strips of matboard and foam center board to this length and to the depth chosen for the other sides. Attach these strips to the frame.

5. The exposed edges of the installed strips create a ledge to hold the backing board. Place the backing board (with objects attached) face down in the frame. Add a filler board. Complete fitting as directed in Basic Fitting Procedure for Wood Frames, steps 5–9 (pages 114–115).

Quick Box for Wood Frames

This is a one-piece unit, cut from a piece of matboard. Careful measurement is important, because the unit must fit almost perfectly into the frame. The objects can be attached to the base of the quick box either before or after the sides of the box are folded and taped (step 5).

1. Lay the frame face down. Measure the depth—it must be deep enough to hold the thickest object, the glazing, and a filler board, plus a little air space between the objects and the glazing. Measure the interior length and width. Add the depth of the thickest object (plus ¼" [6 mm] for air space) to all four sides. In this example, the interior of the frame measures 11" × 14" (27.9 × 35.6 cm), and the thickest object is 1" (2,5 cm), so the board will be cut 13½" × 16½" (34.3 × 41.9 cm).

2. Measure and mark the frame size on the back of the matboard. In this example, mark a 1¼" (3.2 cm) border on all four sides of the board.

3. Score the board on all four marked lines. A score is a cut that slices into the board but does not cut all the way through it. Practice to learn how much pressure is needed to make a score. If the board is accidentally sliced all the way through, the cut can be taped together, but the board is weakened.

4. Cut out and remove the squares of matboard at all four corners. (Objects can be attached at this point if desired.)

5. Fold the sides of the box upward along the score lines. Tape the corners securely on the outside of each corner.

(continued)

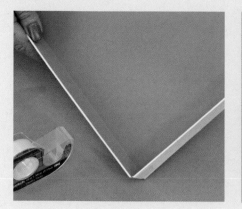

Note: A quick box can be made from foam center board for more strength, but the board must be covered with fabric before cutting or with matboard after cutting unless the surface color of the foam center board is acceptable in the frame design. Measuring can be tricky, because the thickness of the foam center board must be accommodated when adding the depth of the objects to the size of the frame.

6. After all four corners are taped, attach the objects (if not already done in step 4.)

7. Lay the frame face down on the worktable. Place the glazing in the frame. Insert the Quick Box. Complete fitting as directed in Basic Fitting Procedure for Wood Frames, steps 5–9 (pages 114–115).

Lining Metal Frames for Shadow Boxes

The two lining methods described above can be used with metal frames, but the materials must be sized to fit into the channel of the metal frame. A metal frame made to hold art on canvas can be used as a shadow box frame for objects up to about ¾" (1.9 cm) thick. Be sure to allow room for the glazing and backing board when measuring. If using the five-piece lining, attach the strips of foam board/matboard to the sides of the frame using double-sided tape. After the board containing the objects has been inserted in the metal frame, complete the fitting as described in Basic Fitting Procedure for Metal Frames (page 116), steps 4–8. Note: Typical canvas-depth metal frames should only be used for framing lightweight objects, because too much weight exerts pressure on the lower corners of the frame, forcing them to separate. For heavier objects, look for the type of metal frame that has two channels for hardware, one in the front of the frame and one in the back.

The five-piece lining method is used in this canvas-depth metal frame, which will hold a collection of feathers. Notice the blue lining in the frame allows a space at the front for the glazing, and a space at the back for the backing board that will hold the feathers and a filler board. A matboard was used alone for the lining, which is fine for something as light as feathers; for anything heavier, use strips of foam board along with the matboard to create a sturdier ledge.

Other Options for Space in a Shadow Box

Spacer Mats

A group of objects can be surrounded with a window mat. This is often done with seashells, arrowheads, thimbles, military medals, and other small items. The arrangement of the items is determined, then the grouping is measured, and the mat is designed as usual. After the mat is cut and the objects are attached to the backing board, space must be created between the mat and the backing board, lifting the mat away from the objects. This can be done with strips of foam center board cut about ½" (1.3 cm) narrower than the mat borders and attached to the backing board with double-sided tape. Stack more layers if necessary until they are taller than the deepest object; then attach the mat to the top layer of foam center board with double-sided tape. Place the frame face down, insert the glazing, insert the mat/spacer/backing board unit, and complete the fitting as usual. Note: If three or four layers of board are required, the edges of the board will probably be visible beneath the mat when the frame is viewed at an angle. Cover the edges with a strip of matboard the same color as the mat, attached with double-sided tape.

Two layers of foam center board hide beneath the mat and raise it above the surface of the objects in the frame.

FrameSpace

Another option for lining the sides of a shadow box is FrameSpace, plastic strips that can be attached to the rabbet of the frame. There are several sizes providing between ⅛" (3 mm) and ¾" (1.9 cm) of airspace, available in black, white, or clear. Each size has a slot for the glazing, the spacer portion, and a ledge to hold the backing board.

Linen-Covered Liner

Wooden liner frames can be used to create some depth in a shadow box frame, and they take the place of finishing the sides of the frame. The glazing goes in the frame first, then the liner (which has a rabbet), then the backing board with the materials attached, then a backing board.

Clear Framespace has a slot to hold a strip of matboard that will be visible when it is lining the frame.

A wooden liner moulding with a scoop shape was covered with blue fabric to match the backing board in this framing of military medals.

Stapling to the Back of the Frame

This is not a professional technique, but a practical method for the DIY framer. It lets the framer use the full depth of the frame. This is a good, simple option for framing a scrapbook page. It is not appropriate for heavy objects, because the backing is no more than one or two layers of matboard.

1. Lay the frame face down. Measure the full outside size of the frame. Cut the backing board about ¼" (6 mm) short of this size.

2. Clean the interior of the glass and install the glass in the face of the frame using glazier's push points (available at hardware stores and home improvement stores) or other short hardware.

3. Line the sides of the frame with a single layer of matboard that reaches all the way to the back of the frame. Attach the matboard to the frame with double-sided tape and a little white glue.

4. Attach the objects to the backing board. Center the backing board face down on the back of the frame. Add a second layer of matboard for extra strength, if necessary. The edges of the backing boards will be exposed—they can be colored with a felt-tip marker or colored pencil if desired. Use a staple gun to attach the backing to the frame.

5. Install hanging hardware.

Upright Fitting

In most cases, the standard procedure for fitting wood or metal frames can be followed once the lining is in place. Occasionally it is not practical to place the backing board with the objects face down in the frame, perhaps because the hair of a doll or the tassel on a hat may become disheveled in the process. In these rare situations, the fitting can be done with the shadow box standing upright on the worktable—but use a helper to steady the box while you insert the fitting points.

Sink Mat

The sink mat is similar to a spacer mat, except the sink mat closely surrounds and supports a single object. It is a great way to feature an individual item that only needs to be seen from the front, such as a book, magazine, or ceramic tile.

1. Design the framing. Cut a backing board to the outside size of the mat (this board will not be seen in the framing.) Center the object on the backing board.

2. Measure the space (on all four sides) from the edge of the object to the edge of the backing board. Cut strips of foam center board, about ⅛" (3 mm) narrower than the measured space, to surround the object. Attach these strips to the backing board with glue or double-sided tape, aligned with the outer edges of the backing board.

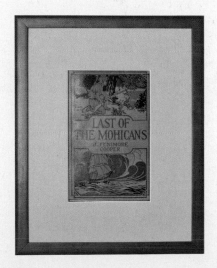

3. Cut more strips, and add a second layer to the backing board. Continue layering until the strips reach the height of the object. If the foam board reaches too high, use matboard strips instead to match the exact height of the object.

4. Cut a window mat that covers the object at least ⅛" (3 mm) on each side. Attach the window mat to the top of the stack of strips with glue or double-sided tape. Place the frame face down on the worktable. Place the glazing in the frame. Insert the sink mat in the frame. Finish the fitting as usual.

FRAMING ART ON PAPER

Types of Art on Paper

The great majority of items that are framed can be called art on paper. Some of the most common types are photographs, art prints, documents, posters, watercolor paintings, drawings, antique prints, children's art, and scrapbook pages. Beyond the common types, many other paper items also find their way into a frame, such as napkins, menus, sheet music, letters, postcards, maps, postage stamps, trading cards, and calendar pages.

Professionals mount art on paper to a backing board. The best method for mounting depends on the type and value of the art.

Measuring Art on Paper

The correct measurements for art on paper depend on the style of framing that will be used: whether the art will be matted, unmatted, or floated, and what part of the image will be visible. The measuring section in Doing the Math in Picture Framing (page 68) offers an extensive discussion of these variations.

Mats and Frames for Art on Paper

Most art on paper should be matted, because it is healthy for the art to have some air space in a frame. However, if framing a calendar page or other decorative art that does not have to be preserved, it is fine to frame without a mat. Glossy photos may stick to the glazing, and thin papers may wrinkle or buckle in the frame if not fully mounted flat. When trimming artwork for framing that will not have a mat, remember the rabbet of the frame will cover about ¼" (6 mm) on all sides.

Almost any type of mat or frame can be used with art on paper because paper is normally thin and lightweight, placing few demands on the framing materials. This leaves the designer free to focus on color, style, and proportion.

If artwork has a cultural or historical tradition that can be used in the framing design, it can add to the overall presentation. Look at Mats and Matboards (page 22) or Designing Framing (page 59) for information about traditions in framing.

The mat colors in this design coordinate with the colors in the art, while the simple line of the frame complements the style of the art.

Oriental scroll proportions were used to accent the long, vertical shape of this art on paper.

Glazing for Art on Paper

The surface of paper is fragile, so all types of art on paper should be protected with glazing. Any type of glass or acrylic may be used. Although glass is by far the most common glazing, acrylic may be preferred in a playroom or children's bedroom, to avoid issues with broken glass.

Some designers like the look of art pressed between two sheets of glass so that the wall color or wallpaper pattern shows around the art. This is not healthy for the art unless spacers are used. See Fitting (page 111) for information about this technique.

Tips for framing specific types of art on paper are offered later in this chapter.

Acrylic is used as the glazing on this map, which hangs in an office cubicle that cannot support a lot of weight; acrylic is about half the weight of glass.

Attachments

Attaching the art safely and securely in the frame is one of the most important parts of framing. Poor adhesives and improper attachments are the most common cause of damage to art on paper caused by picture framing.

Amateurs and beginning framers often attach artwork to the mat opening, but professionals attach art to the backing board because this board is solid and sturdy, while the window mat is weakened by the hole cut out of it. The backing board should be of equal or better quality than the matboard, because the back of the art will be in continuous full contact with this board.

Here's how to position art on a backing board: Lay the art on the backing board. Place the mat on top of the art. Arrange the art in the mat opening until it is positioned just right. Place a clean weight on the art (framers use such things as paper weights or small sacks of marbles) and carefully remove the mat. Attach the art to the backing board.

A juice glass serves as a weight to hold the print in place, ready to be attached to the backing board.

Standard Materials and Methods and When to Use Them

The standard attachment methods discussed in this section are for decorative art only. Although all of the suggested materials are of good quality, the adhesives are difficult to remove from the art without any damage or residue remaining, so they are unsuitable for conservation framing.

Taping

Single-sided Adhesive Tape. Use ordinary Magic Mending Tape. Use one or two small single strips across the top similar to the size of hinges. Do not run the tape across the entire length; over time it will cause a ruffling of the paper directly beneath the taped area.

Double-sided Tape. This may be used for floating decorative art on a backing board; the art may be damaged during possible future removal. Use a strip near the center top, or two strips evenly distributed for long horizontal art.

Two postcards of Impressionist art paintings are floated on a piece of blue matboard using double-sided tape and then fitted in a ready-made mat and frame.

Art should be suspended from one or two pieces of tape at the top, so it can move slightly in response to changes in the environment.

Do not restrict paper with tape placed on all four sides, because the art will buckle during changes in humidity.

Full Mounting

In full mounting, the entire back of the art is adhered to a support board. This is considered a permanent alteration of the art, so it is not appropriate for valuable pieces. Full mounting is useful for decorative art such as large posters that might slump if framed without support, and for art that will hang in humid areas where moisture could cause buckling. Use a sturdy board such as matboard, illustration board, or foam center board. Check the board for dents, because imperfections will be visible in the surface of the art after mounting. If you find it difficult to position the art perfectly on the board, use an oversized board and trim it to exact size after mounting.

Full mounting is a complete attachment of the art to a backing board. It is only appropriate for decorative art. This print will hang in a bathroom; it has been fully mounted to prevent the paper from buckling when the room gets steamy.

Pressure-sensitive Mounting

Use a board precoated with adhesive (or cover a board with a sheet of double-stick adhesive).

1. Lay the board on a flat work surface. Along the top edge of the board, peel back an inch (centimeter) or two of the cover sheet that protects the adhesive. Align the top of the print with the top edge of the board, and press it onto the adhesive.

2. Continue to peel back the cover sheet a few inches (centimeters) at a time, allowing the art to fall onto the adhesive. Smooth the art frequently, removing any air pockets—be firm, but do not press hard because the art may stretch or wrinkle.

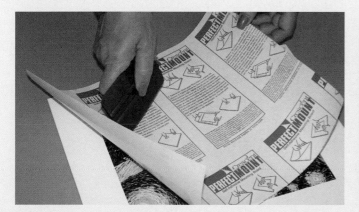

3. Place the release paper on top of the art. Lightly but evenly burnish over the entire surface of the art.

Note: Follow the manufacturer's instructions, which may include laying the finished mounting face up under a weight (such as matboard with books on top) for a period of time to allow the adhesive to set.

Spray Mounting

Spray mounting is an acceptable method for the DIY framer. It does not provide the permanence of professional heat or vacuum mounting, but it is a practical alternative. Choose a spray made for mounting paper. Work on sheets of newspaper or some other disposable surface that can contain the overspray. Control the fumes with good ventilation. Follow the manufacturer's instructions for application of adhesive, which typically suggests spraying both the art and the board for best adhesion. For large pieces, roll the artwork, match the top of the art to the top of the board, and unroll the art gradually, smoothing the art as it makes contact with the adhesive. Practice first with kraft paper. Some spray adhesives are repositionable for a short time, allowing portions of the artwork to be carefully lifted and re-smoothed to remove air bubbles.

Archival Materials and Methods

Archival attachments are important for any valued art; the value may be historic, sentimental, or monetary, or a combination of those elements.

Hinges

Hinges are the preferred professional method for attaching valued paper items to a backing board. A small amount of adhesive makes contact with the art, but the adhesive is reversible with water and does not leave harmful residue on the art. Make hinges using Japanese paper and starch paste, or purchase a roll of hinging tape that is already coated with starch adhesive. See Tools of the Trade (page 42) for further information.

If making your own hinges, the first step is to tear the Japanese paper into strips. The strips are torn, rather than cut, to create soft, feathery edges that grip the adhesive. The strips for a typical hinge are about ½" (1.3 cm) to 1" (2.5 cm) wide. To tear the strips, place a ruler about ½" (1.3 cm) from the edge of the paper. Dip a small brush into clean water, and draw the brush along the edge of the ruler. Place one hand on the ruler, and use the other to pull the ½" (1.3 cm)-wide strip of paper away from the ruler, creating a ragged, feathery edge.

If using starch paste that needs to be cooked, prepare it in advance so that it can cool. If using pre-pasted hinging paper, have a small bowl of clean water on the worktable. You will also need a small brush to attach the paste or water to the hinges.

You use Japanese paper and starch paste like a piece of tape by just laying the art on the backing board and applying pasted strips that attach the top edge of the art to the board. For many DIY purposes, this may be appropriate. It does create a water-reversible, archival-quality attachment. However, museum conservators and professional conservation framers prefer the T-hinge, which attaches to the back of the art.

This is an acceptable method for attaching art to a backing board using paste and Japanese paper, but conservators prefer an attachment method that does not allow adhesive to touch the face of the art.

Mounting Strips/Mounting Corners

Mounting strips and mounting corners are "independent supports," meaning they do not attach to the art but simply support it, while an adhesive backing attaches them to the backing board. This makes them an excellent choice for conservation framing, as long as the supports are acid-free and made from archival-quality materials. The placement and number of supports depends on the size of the art. An 8" x 10" (20.3 x 25.4 cm) photo can easily be held with four mounting corners, while a 16" x 20" (40.6 x 50.8 cm) photo needs the support of a mounting strip centered on each of the four sides. A mat can be cut with an opening that hides all of the supports.

For this small print, a single mounting strip at the bottom and two mounting corners at the top provide sufficient support. Do not tightly restrict the art—allow a small amount of "wiggle room" for expansion and contraction of the art during changes in temperature and humidity.

The T-Hinge

This is the classic conservation hinge. It has two parts: a tab attached to the back of the art, and a crosspiece that bonds the tab to the backing board. The number of hinges depends on the size of the art; two hinges are used on most pieces.

1. Tear two pieces of Japanese paper, one 2" x ½" (5.1 x 1.3 cm), the other 3" x ½" (7.6 x 1.3 cm).

2. Using a small brush, apply a small amount of starch paste to the lower edge of the 2" piece of paper, which is the hinge. If using prepasted paper, moisten the lower edge.

3. Apply the hinge to the top edge of the back of the art, near the corner.

4. Cover the hinge with a piece of cotton blotter paper, and place a weight over the paper until the adhesive is dry, about ten minutes.

5. When the hinges are dry, position the art on the backing board.

6. Apply a small amount of paste to the entire surface of one side of the 3" (7.6 cm) piece of paper, which is the crosspiece.

7. Cover each hinge with a crosspiece, placing the crosspieces just above the top edge of the art; gently tap them to smooth them.

8. Cover the hinges with piece of plastic sheet or blotter paper and place under a weight until dry. Smooth stones were used here as weights.

The Float Hinge

This hinge is used for valued art that will "float" on a backing board with the edges of the art exposed in the framing. This is also called a pass-through hinge. The size and number of the hinges depend on the size and weight of the art; two hinges are used on most pieces.

1. Apply a small amount of paste to the lower third of a Japanese paper hinge (or moisten the lower third of pre-pasted hinge paper), and attach it to the back of the art, about 2" (5.1 cm) from the top edge of the art. Cover the hinge with blotter paper, add a weight, and allow it to dry.

2. Repeat step 1 until all hinges are attached. Position the art on the backing board. With a pencil, mark the placement for each hinge on the board.

3. Using a craft knife or mat cutter, cut horizontal slits in the board at the pencil marks. The slits should be a little wider than the hinges.

4. Pass the hinges through the slits.

5. Adjust the position of the art as needed, then secure each hinge to the backing board with a crosspiece.

6. Cover the hinge with cotton paper and a weight until dry.

Note: Up or down? After the hinge paper is passed through the slits in the matboard, should it be placed upward, toward the top of the matboard, or folded downward? Opinions differ, because there are beneficial aspects to both methods. In our demonstration above, the hinge was folded downward, but many framers believe that upward is better, especially for heavy art papers.

Z-Hinge

The lower corners of floated art may lean forward or curl toward the glass. A z-hinge controls this movement. Apply one z-hinge at each lower corner.

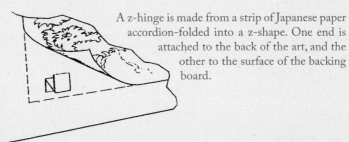

A z-hinge is made from a strip of Japanese paper accordion-folded into a z-shape. One end is attached to the back of the art, and the other to the surface of the backing board.

Encapsulation

Encapsulation uses sheets of clear, flexible film and double-sided tape to encase fragile paper in a protective package. Use a conservation film such as polyester or polypropylene, which are acid-free and inert (they will not change or release art-harming gasses). Many photo album pages are made of suitable material, or envelopes of film made especially for preserving artwork can be purchased from some craft and hobby stores and from conservation suppliers online. The encapsulation package is ready to frame, and can be attached to the backing board with tape or corner pockets. The mat opening can be designed to cover the edges of the artwork or show the edges, whichever is preferred.

1. Cut two pieces of film about 2" (5.1 cm) larger than the artwork. Place the artwork on the work-table, and lay one piece of film centered on top of the art.

2. Apply a strip of double-sided tape to the film, about ¼" (6 mm) away from all sides of the artwork. Place a very thin strip of acid-free paper along the top edge of the bottom strip of tape. This prevents the art from touching adhesive. Remove the artwork from beneath the film, and place it on top of the film, just above the strip of paper, centered between the tape strips at the sides.

3. Place the second piece of film on top of the first. The alignment need not be perfect, but the two pieces of film must be smooth with no buckling. Burnish the tape strips with the side of a bone folder or the back of a spoon.

Deacidification of Paper

Deacidification is a conservation process that literally means what it says: A solution is sprayed onto paper to neutralize the acids present in the paper and provide a buffer for acids encountered in the future. This slows yellowing and prevents embrittlement for many years. Used by frame shops and museums, this technique is also available for the DIY framer, because the spray is sold in craft and hobby stores for use in paper crafts, such as card making and scrapbooking. It is useful for preserving newspapers, kids' art on construction paper, antique prints, and other acidic papers. Do not use on glossy papers, because the spray does not penetrate the gloss finish. Although the deacidification spray usually makes no visible change to the art, be sure to read any disclaimers on the package of the spray, and always test the product on a corner of the art before spraying it on the entire sheet.

A deacidification spray neutralizes the acids in paper, dramatically slowing deterioration.

Fitting Art on Paper

The process of finishing the framing (installing all of the materials in the frame, sealing it up, and adding hanging hardware) is called fitting. See Fitting (page 111) for step-by-step instructions.

Special Handling Tips for Art on Paper

Limited Edition Print

A mat should be cut that allows the entire sheet of paper to be maintained in its original state. Some prints become highly collectible, and the ones that are in prime original condition are the most valuable.

Giclées. The term "giclée" refers to a printing process used to make detailed, richly colored limited edition prints using very sophisticated ink-jet printers. The printing may be done on paper or canvas of various types and sizes. Framing should follow the form of the print: A giclée on paper should be framed like other limited edition prints on paper, while a giclée on canvas should be framed like other art on canvas.

Giclée

Diplomas and Certificates. Take good care of the important ones, because they may not be replaceable. Use mats or spacers to keep them away from the glazing.

Diploma

Limited Edition Prints. A limited edition print is a fine-quality printed image that is limited to a pre-selected number. The artist who created the original piece of art signs and numbers each print. The artist's signature is typically on the lower right portion of blank paper just below the printed art. The print's edition number is usually opposite the signature at the lower left. This information is meant to show in the framing, so the measurement for the mat opening should include as much of the paper as necessary to expose the name and number, plus some plain paper at the sides and top of the printed image for balance. The amount of paper at the top and sides may be equal to the amount shown at the bottom, or, if that seems like too much, show just ¼" (6 mm) on a small print or ½" (1.3 cm) to 1" (2.5 cm) on a large print. DO NOT trim the excess paper surrounding the printed image, even though it might be tempting if there is a lot of paper—any alteration of the original condition of a limited edition print negatively affects its value. The excess paper should not be folded, either (folded is considered damaged, but to a lesser degree than trimmed).

Reproductions. Also called "open edition prints," these images are produced in large numbers and not signed by the artist. This includes posters and most of the art prints bought in craft stores and online. Although there is no need to show the white paper edge around the printed image, sometimes ¼" (6 mm) of this border makes an attractive accent. Reproductions can be framed without mats if they are just decorative prints that do not need to be preserved.

Reproduction

Scrapbook Pages. Treat these like art on paper if the work is relatively flat, or use shadow box framing if there are dimensional components. Photos and decorative elements may not be attached well and may dangle when placed vertically in a frame. This may be a good project to use the Stapling to the Back of the Frame method (page 126) described in Fitting.

Scrapbook Page

Newspaper Clippings. Place against a dark background (gray, brown, or black) to minimize show-through from printing on the reverse side of the clipping. Newspaper will turn yellow, so make a copy of the clipping and frame the copy if you prefer it to stay white. If you want to frame the original, deacidification will help a lot but will not prevent all discoloration.

Newspaper Clipping

Brass Rubbings. These are usually made with a waxy crayon on thin black or off-white paper, which often gets wrinkled during the rubbing process. They can be hinged at the top like other paper art, if the wrinkled paper is acceptable. If you want the piece to lie flat, the paper can be spray-mounted to a matboard or foam center board; or a sticky-board may be used, but this type of full mounting is not appropriate if the rubbing is valuable.

Brass Rubbing

Art with Special Edges. The float method is used when you want to show all of the edges of the art in the framing. This is common with art that has "deckled" edges (a jagged, torn appearance), with papyrus paintings, and with art that continues to the edges of the paper. The art is attached to the backing board using a float hinge. The mat opening should be between ½" (1.3 cm) and 2" (5.1 cm) larger than the outer measurement of the artwork, depending on the size of the art and the amount of the backing board you want to show. The color of the backing board is an important part of the visual design, because it is the defining line directly surrounding the art.

Art with Special Edges

Photographs. There are more types of photographs printed on more types of paper than ever before, from heirloom antiques to a print made at the drug store yesterday. The chemical properties of the numerous different photo processes have unique qualities that age differently. Some fade or discolor from internal changes that will occur whether the photo is on display or stored in a box. Others change when exposed to light. Because it is now quick and inexpensive to scan and print a copy of any treasured photograph, it is recommended to use a copy for framing and store the original in a dry, dark place. Glossy photo finishes—and some matte finishes—may stick to the glazing (to glass more readily than to acrylic), so use mats or spacers on glossy photos.

Fine art photography may carry the photographer's signature on the mat, rather than on the photograph. Photographs are typically printed without enough blank border to contain the signature, and photographers hesitate to sign their name on top of the photo image. Signing the mat (and numbering, if the edition is limited) is the somewhat awkward compromise that has become common practice. Frame these photos with the mat as is, or add a top mat with an opening that exposes the photographer's signature.

Photographs

Drawings (Pastel, Pencil, Pen, and Ink).

The mat opening varies, depending on the artist's work—some drawings are contained with obvious edges; some sprawl. Pastel and pencil drawings have loose media on the surface that can be smeared, and particles may come loose in the framing. A spacer mat hidden beneath the top mat will catch and hide these particles. Simply cut a mat with an opening ½" (1.3 cm) larger than the opening in the top mat,

and attach it to the underside of the top mat. Do not use acrylic glazing on a pastel, as the static tends to pull particles from the art.

Drawing

Collages (Fine Art Collage, Embellished Book Pages, and so on).

These assemblages of paper and embellishments may be almost flat, or thick and dimensional. The amount of dimension determines the special needs of the framing. A thin collage can be framed like typical art on paper, with enough mats to keep the glazing from touching the art. Thick collages need to be treated as shadow box projects.

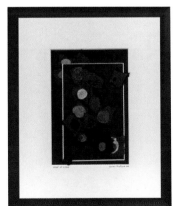
Collage

Decorative Posters.

Often people do not want to put a mat on posters, because they do not want to increase the size. But, if not supported with a mat, large paper will slump or buckle when framed. Full mounting is one effective solution. Decorative posters are prone to fading from exposure to light, so use ultraviolet-filtering glazing if the poster is intended to last for many years.

Decorative Poster

Papyrus Paintings.

Many people like to float this art on a matboard, so they can see all the uneven edges that are part of the beauty of a real piece of woven papyrus. Gummed adhesives, such as Lineco's gummed linen tape, can be used to make pass-through hinges that will hold well.

Papyrus Painting

Children's Art. Wax crayon, flaky tempera paint, finger paint, layers of paper glued together—children's art encompasses a world of possibilities. Much of it is done on newsprint, construction paper, poster board, even paper plates—all great for crafts but not made to last. It is wonderful to support and encourage budding artists, and framing a special piece is one great way to do that. Acrylic box frames or metal frames that can be opened to change the art are a good option. If a treasured piece will be displayed for many years, use ultraviolet-filtering glazing to help minimize fading caused by exposure to light.

Children's Art

Postage Stamps. If the stamps are purely decorative, it is okay to use the stamp adhesive to attach the stamps to a matboard. For any stamp of value, encase it in a stamp mount, available at local coin and stamp shops or online. They are small, clear, stamp-sized envelopes that may have an adhesive back for attachment to a matboard.

Postage Stamps

Watercolor Paintings. Watercolor paintings may be done on thick paper, which requires strong attachment to the backing board. Watercolor paper is sometimes buckled (deep ripples caused by wetness during painting). It can be very difficult to flatten these paintings. To protect its value, original art should not be fully mounted. A watercolor should be hinged to the backing board and matted to keep it from touching the glass. A deep mat can be added to a buckled watercolor which will enhance the look of the authentic character. Some of the paints are prone to fading and can benefit from the protection of ultraviolet-filtering glazing.

Watercolor Painting

Antique Papers (Foxing and Other Damage). Many antique papers (documents, book plates, hand-colored engravings, and so on) display rust-colored dots or splotches. This is called "foxing" and is believed to come from minerals lodged in the paper during manufacturing. It may be corrected by experts but should not be attempted by amateurs. Antique papers may be yellowed and have stains and other marks. Most antique prints are framed with all of their signs of aging intact, considered part of the authentic character of the print. Some printing inks and paints used in hand-coloring are prone to fading, so use ultraviolet-filtering glazing to provide some protection.

Antique Paper

FRAMING ART ON CANVAS

Types of Art on Canvas

Oil paintings (and, more recently, acrylic paintings) are the traditional version of art on canvas, with paint directly applied to a prepared piece of linen or cotton fabric stretched over a frame of wooden bars. Prints on canvas are a popular modern variation, with art images either directly printed onto canvas or separately printed and mounted to canvas (so the woven texture of the fabric shows through the art). The prints are then stretched onto wooden bars and coated with a glossy or semi-glossy finish to be displayed like oil paintings. These prints may be limited edition giclée prints or mass-produced open edition prints.

Oil and acrylic paintings have visible brushstrokes, which may be almost smooth or thick and dimensional. The visible brushstrokes are part of the appeal of art on canvas, so transparent mock brushstrokes are often used to embellish art prints on canvas. If done well, it can be hard to tell the difference between these embellished prints and true paintings, but on close inspection it is possible to see whether the brushstrokes are a clear overlay or actually colored paints. In a few instances, colors of paint have been used to hand-embellish. Very rarely, colors of paint are used to embellish limited edition giclées on canvas.

There are several ways to create art on canvas. A giclée on canvas is produced by directly printing onto fabric.

Designing Framing for Art on Canvas

Measuring Art on Canvas

The size of the image is usually obvious, with distinct rectangular borders. The size of the frame is usually the size of the image. There is a contemporary exception, in which the art image is wrapped around the support bars and hung on the wall without a frame. A canvas that will be presented in this "gallery wrap" style must be measured to account for the wrapped sides, which is further discussed in Stretching Art on Canvas (page 146).

The canvas usually does not expand more than a fraction of an inch during stretching, so the image can be measured flat, without pulling. If the fabric seems to have a lot of elasticity (as is the case with some prints on canvas), gently pull the fabric while measuring. At least ½" (1.3 cm) of canvas is needed for stretching on a wooden stretcher frame, and more is better. In most cases, there is plenty of excess canvas to use.

Frames for Art on Canvas

Ornate gilded frames are the time-honored favorite for traditional oil paintings, but today's variety of art calls for a variety of frame styles, and any frame that suits the art is appropriate for art on canvas. Because the wooden bars that support the canvas are thick, it looks best to frame art on canvas in a frame with a deep rabbet, or in a wide frame that hides the protruding bars in a shadow behind the frame. If a narrow, shallow frame is used, the bars look obvious, even if covered with a dust cover, which does not look attractive when hanging on the wall.

The "floater frame" is a style made especially for art on canvas. The stretched canvas is mounted onto a ledge at the back of the frame so that the sides of the canvas are somewhat visible. The canvas may be stretched in the gallery wrap style (the painted canvas wraps around the sides of the stretcher bars), or the canvas may be stretched in the traditional style (the full painting shows from the front), and the sides of the canvas may be covered with black tape.

Both of these treatments work well on the oil painting. Which is best depends on the room where the painting will hang and the preference of the designer.

A floater frame has a recessed ledge made to hold a stretched canvas. The canvas can be attached to the frame using strips of adhesive-backed hook-and-loop tape.

Borders for Art on Canvas

If a border is desired between the frame and the canvas, liners are used instead of ordinary mats. The most common liner is a flat or sloping wood moulding about 1" (2.5 cm) wide, covered with white or off-white linen. Liner moulding has a rabbet; the liner rabbet size is the measurement used for the art, glazing, and other materials that will fit in the frame.

There are ready-made frames in standard sizes for art on canvas, and many of these have a liner of this type, perhaps with a small gold fillet as well. Liners can be purchased in custom sizes from several online sources, or in sticks to be cut and built by the framer. It can be tricky to know what size of outer frame is needed for a liner, because of that extra allowance that should be part of every frame, including the liner frame. It is tempting to simply assume the frame size will need to be ⅛" (3 mm) larger than the liner size, but it is best to order or build the liner first and measure its actual size before ordering or building the frame.

This oil painting is bordered by a linen-covered wooden liner.

Glazing for Art on Canvas

As was mentioned in the introduction (page 6) to this book, there are sometimes disagreements among professional framers about the "right way" or "best way" to do something. Whether or not paintings on canvas need to be covered with glass is one area of disagreement.

Traditionally, paintings on canvas were oil paintings. When completely dry, an oil painting was coated with varnish, so any dirt that landed on the painting was attached to the layer of varnish. When the painting became soiled and began to look yellowed or dirty, the varnish was removed and replaced with fresh varnish, making the painting look as good as new. Because the varnish protected the painting, no glass was needed in the frame, allowing the texture of the oil paint brushstrokes to be enjoyed by viewers of the art.

Putting glass on oil paintings is a relatively modern idea used by some museums and picture framers to protect the art from surface damage and air pollution.

Museums are using glass to prevent damage but many traditional framers still maintain that oil paintings should generally be framed without glass in home environments. Today, art on canvas may include many things besides oil paintings: acrylic paintings, mixed media, an art print or photograph that has been printed on fabric, or an art print that has been "transferred" to canvas. Modern paintings may or may not have a protective varnish finish; even if they do, it may not be removable. The surface of today's art on canvas may be fragile and difficult to clean or to repair. Also, although traditional oil paints and acrylic paints are not prone to fading from exposure to light, some of the newer types of art on canvas can benefit from the protection of ultraviolet-filtering glazing.

So, glazing or no glazing for art on canvas? As with many framing decisions, it is a matter of personal preference. If glazing is used on a canvas, space must be provided between the art and the glazing. See Fitting Art on Canvas (page 120) for a discussion of spacing options.

Stretching Art on Canvas

Like needlework, art on canvas must be made smooth and rigid before framing. Stretching the canvas on stretcher bars is the most common method. Stretcher bars are strips of flat, lightweight wood with a tongue-and-groove miter at each end, which allow them to easily interlock with another strip. They are used to make a frame for stretching needlepoint or art on canvas. Stretcher bars are typically sold as individual strips in whole inch sizes in the most common standard sizes and a few others. To make a stretcher frame, four strips are required, two of the length size and two of the width size. They are sold in art supply stores and some craft stores, and a wide variety of sizes is available online. To assemble, simply bring two corners together and work them into one another until joined, and then repeat with the other three corners. Gently tap with a hammer if necessary to complete the join.

Some framers and conservators worry that the acids in the wooden stretcher bars could damage the canvas. To protect valuable art on canvas, seal the bars before stretching with a coat of acrylic medium from an art supply store, or cover them with Lineco's Frame Sealing Tape.

Choosing the Size of the Bars

In most cases, the size of the painted image will be the size of the stretcher bars. If the designer wants the image to wrap around the sides of the bars (gallery wrap style) so the canvas can hang alone without a frame, use the following method: Measure the depth of the stretcher bar, double that measurement to account for both sides, and subtract that amount from the length and width of the image to determine the size of the bars. Stretching requires at least ½" (1.3 cm) of excess canvas on all four sides, so be sure there is a minimum of ½" (1.3 cm) available.

The mitered, tongue-and-groove ends of stretcher bars are designed to fit firmly into one another.

Just work the corners of stretcher bars together, pushing and adjusting as necessary.

Canvas panels come in standard sizes and are about ⅛" (3 mm) thick. This view of the back of three boards shows that new boards are usually bright white, while older student-grade boards may become yellowed from acids in the board. Canvas board is rigid and ready to frame without stretching.

The Stretching Process

These are the materials needed to stretch an oil painting on canvas. Use a staple gun and stainless steel staples to attach the canvas to the stretcher bars; do not use tacks that make large holes in the canvas and may rust. Canvas pliers are necessary to hold and pull the canvas during stretching.

1. Assemble the stretcher bars. Check the squareness.

2. Measure to find the middle of each side of the canvas and the stretcher bars, and mark with a pencil.

3. Match up the pencil marks on the short sides of the canvas and stretcher bars.

(continued)

4. Fold the material over one of the short sides of the frame and fasten in the center with a staple.

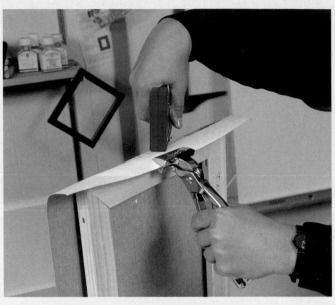

5. Reverse to the opposite side. Holding the edge of the canvas with canvas (it is difficult to get a firm grip and appropriate pull with any other tool), stretch until the canvas is taut; staple in the center, matching pencil marks. Pull just until the fabric is taut; too much tension can cause ink or paint to split.

6. Turn the frame so one of the longer sides is up. Grip and pull until diagonal wrinkles appear from the first two staples to the point where it is stretching; staple in the center. Repeat on the fourth side, pulling material until a diamond-shaped set of four wrinkles forms, and staple at the center.

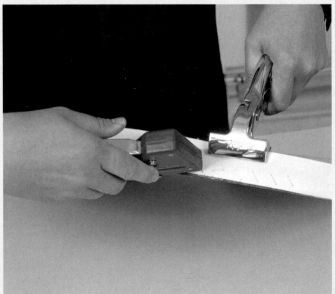

7. Move pliers a couple inches to the left of the center staples and staple again. Repeat in the same direction, stapling every inch or two, working to the corner of the frame. Now do the same from the center to the right, but stop about 3" (7.6 cm) from the corner. Do the same on the opposite long side, then on the two short sides.

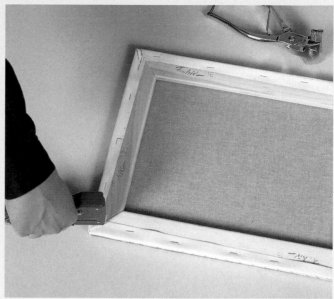

8. Finish the corners last, folding the material under itself and pulling it snug. Staple securely.

9. After stretching, there is typically excess fabric on the back of the stretcher bars. With original art, all of this is left in place, to follow the conservation practice of keeping original art unchanged. A few staples can be used to secure the excess fabric to the back of the stretcher bars. For decorative art, trimming is acceptable.

Fitting Art on Canvas

The process of finishing the framing (installing all of the materials in the frame, sealing it up, and adding hanging hardware) is called fitting. See Fitting (page 111) for step-by-step instructions. Note the tips about filler board and sealing wood frame interiors (page 113).

About Corner Keys

Manufactured stretcher bars often come with triangular wooden or plastic "corner keys." They are designed to fit into the slots in the interior corners of the stretcher after the canvas has been stretched, to create a tighter stretch that can be tightened even more in the future by tapping the keys further into the slots. There is much debate about the use of keys. Some believe they offer an effective way to maintain a taut canvas, but others have observed that the keys disfigure the canvas over time by pushing out the corners.

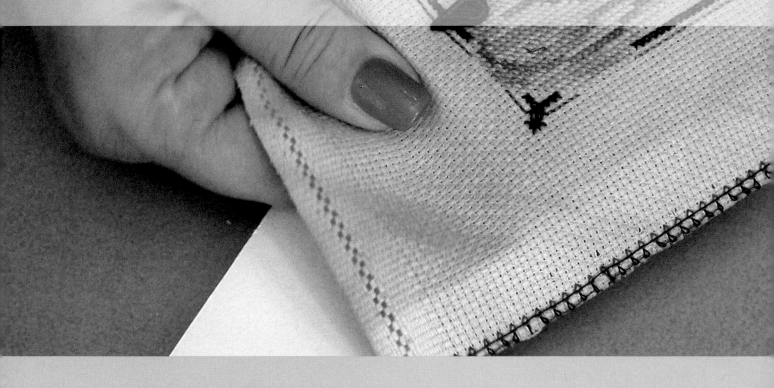

FRAMING NEEDLEWORK AND FABRIC

Types of Needlework

The term "needlework" refers to a broad range of crafts typically made with some type of woven fabric, some type of thread or cord, and some type of needle or needle-like tool. Any type of needlework can be framed. This chapter deals with the types that are basically flat, such as counted cross-stitch, needlepoint, embroidery, a crocheted doily, or an individual quilt block. Dimensional needlework pieces, such as a knitted baby sweater, are treated like objects in picture framing, so they are discussed in Shadow Boxes (page 162).

Glazing protects needlework from dust and airborne pollutants. Matting keeps the glazing away from the surface of the needlework.

Designing Framing for Needlework

Measuring Needlework

Determine what should show in the frame or mat opening. Sometimes there is an obvious border, or perhaps it would look better to show an extra ¼" (6 mm) of the needlework fabric all around the work. Perhaps the cross-stitch bouquet would look best with an inch (2.5 cm) of fabric surrounding it, or maybe the frame should come close to the stitching. Pull the work taut (to the point of tension, but not tight) when measuring.

Mats and Frames for Needlework

Needlework pieces can be matted and framed just like art on paper. If the needlework will be matted, determine the color and size just as with other types of art. Paper surface mats are fine, but professional framers like to use fabric-covered mats on needlework because the texture and richness of color are compatible with the character of the needlework. Any style of frame that looks appropriate with the needlework may be used, as long as it is deep enough to hold the framing materials.

Floating Needlework

Delicate antique fabric, or any fabric with interesting edges, can be "floated" on a backing board to show all of the fabric. The needlework can be sewn to a matboard covered with linen or other fabric, or to a plain matboard, and then a mat can be cut with an opening that allows all of the needlework to show. If not using a mat, a spacer can be hidden in the rabbet of the frame to keep the glazing from touching the art and to provide necessary air circulation. When floating artwork, the board the art rests on is a visible part of the framing design.

Archival Considerations

Needlework is usually pretty durable, but fabric is susceptible to damage from acids and adhesives, so be sure to keep those bad influences away from direct contact with the work. Air circulation in the frame is also important, so always use mats or spacers on valuable needlework that will be covered with glazing.

This cross-stitch was framed using a fabric-covered mat that matches the needlework fabric.

Glazing for Needlework

With needlework, the decision to use glazing or not depends partly on the framing. Paper surface mats need to be covered by glass or acrylic, because the surface is easily scratched or spotted and may even warp on a very humid day. Unmatted or fabric-matted needlework does not have to be glazed, but that means the surface of the work is exposed. This can be hazardous to the needlework if there is cigarette or fireplace smoke, kitchen grease, or sprayed cleaning fluids in the room. In the absence of airborne pollutants, unglazed needleworks can remain in very good condition for decades, until ordinary household dust takes a toll, at which time the needlework can be removed for professional cleaning. Fabric-covered mats can be brushed clean of dust (as can the needlework): The fabric creates a sturdy board—it is not completely invulnerable but is stronger than ordinary paper surface mats.

Traditional wool needlepoint is often not glazed, and the same is true for unmatted counted cross-stitch, but this is a decision best made on a piece-by-piece basis. If an unmatted needlework has glazing, there must be a spacer between the work and the glazing. Needlework sealed in a frame with no air space encourages mold and mildew during humid weather, and oils from wool threads can cause a haze on the glazing.

This fragile antique embroidery is protected by glass; the mat provides air space in the frame and keeps the glass from touching the needlework.

Embellished Needlework

Needlework may be embellished with dimensional objects such as beads or ribbons. To protect the decorative elements, the needlework may be framed without glazing, or, if glazing is preferred, mats and/or spacers can be used to keep the glazing away from the surface of the work. Be careful not to pull too hard when stretching embellished needlework, as the decoration may become distorted.

Beads embellish this needlework.

Stretching Needlework

Before it can be framed, needlework must be pulled and held taut, or it will be wrinkled and askew in the framing. The pulling and holding process is called "stretching." There are several methods for stretching needlework. The goal when stretching is to pull the work taut but not tight; the difference between the two is the degree of tension involved: The needlework should be straight, square, and secure, but it should not be put under undue strain. There is normally excess fabric around the design work to allow for the stretching process; about ½" (1.3 cm) or so is needed per side. If there is not enough on one or all sides, a strip of cotton fabric can be sewn to the edge of the needlework (by hand or machine) to create sufficient excess.

The color of the backing board may show through lightweight needlework and affect its appearance, so test the backing board with the needlework before stretching. The color can be altered by adhering a piece of appropriate color matboard to the surface of the backing board before stretching.

Some needlework artists like to have their needlework padded, which gives a softer, rounded shape to the stretched piece. To pad a needlework, place a layer or two of polyester batting (the flat type used in quilting, not the loose fiberfill for stuffing pillows) on the support board before stretching the needlework. Attach the batting to the board with a piece of double-sided tape to prevent shifting.

Needlepoint is handled differently from other types of needlework, so it is separately discussed later in the chapter (Designing Framing for Needlepoint, page 160).

Stretching Methods

There are numerous methods for stretching needlework; the methods described here are practical for the DIY framer. In stretching, the needlework will be attached to a backing board, often foam board. Before stretching, the backing board must be cut to size. To determine the size, the designer must first decide how much of the fabric to show around the work, and whether or not the work will be matted.

This crewel work was stretched on an off-white board similar to the color of the needlework fabric.

Tight Fit

This method uses pressure alone to hold the needlework square and taut. It provides a level area around the needlework for work that will be matted.

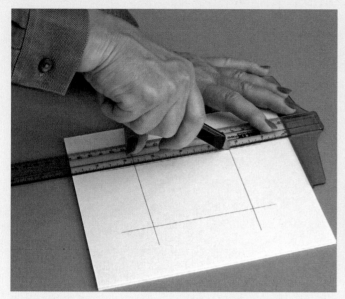

1. Determine the size of the mat opening and mat borders. Cut a piece of foam board to the outer size of the mat, and mark the mat opening in its correct position on the foam board. Using a craft knife, cut out the center of the board along the marked lines. Use a straight cut, and do not stray inside the lines.

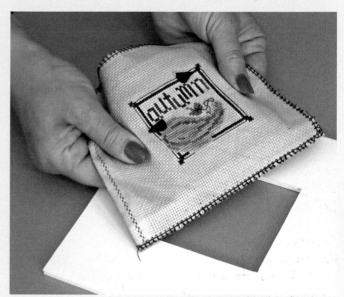

2. Center the needlework on the cutout piece of foam board.

3. Replace the foam board "window," easing it over the needlework. If the fit is too tight because the needlework fabric is too thick, trim the cutout piece of foam board a bit and try again.

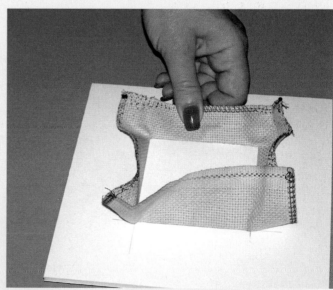

4. From the back of the board, pull the excess fabric as necessary to adjust the needlework until it is taut and straight. Use a couple of angled straight pins to hold excess fabric in place on the back of the board.

Pinning

This is probably the favorite method of professional framers, especially for counted cross-stitch. Using foam board as a backing, the needlework is wrapped around the board, and stainless steel ballpoint pins hold the fabric in place. These pins slide between the fibers of the needlework rather than break them as sharp pins can. This method can be used for stretching silk scarves and other fabric items.

1. Cut a piece of foam board to the visual size of the needlework—the size that will be seen in the mat or frame. Measure and mark the center of the board and the needlework on all four sides. Use a water-removable pencil or marker (the kind used in quilting) to mark the fabric, or use pins.

2. Place the needlework face up on the board. At the center of the top, stick a pin through the fabric into the edge (the core) of the foam board—not all the way; let the pinhead stick out for now. Move to the opposite side (center bottom), pull the fabric taut and insert a pin part way. Do the same on the two sides.

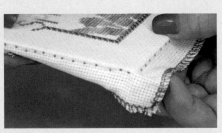

3. Working from the center of each side to the corners, place a pin about every ¼" (6 mm) to ½" (1.3 cm). Be sure to keep the grain of the fabric straight. Pin all four sides, coming to within about ¼" (6 mm) of the corners.

4. When satisfied with the stretch, push the pins into the foam board until the head of each pin rests snugly against the fabric.

5. Fold the corners neatly, with the excess fabric at the back of the board, and tack with a pin. Secure the loose fabric on the back by inserting a few pins at an angle to penetrate the board, but do not pierce the front.

Tight Fit with Pinning

If matting will be used with a pinned needlework, the tight fit method can be used: Mark the size of the mat opening, cut and remove the foam board cutout, trim the cutout to allow for the pin heads that will be on all four sides, and then use the cutout to stretch the needlework using the pinning method. When pinning is complete, replace the foam board "window" to make a level surface for the mat.

An example of combining the tight fit with pinning, this cross-stitch was pinned to the foam board cutout and then inserted into the foam board border.

Lacing

This is a time-honored, traditional method for stretching needlework. It is also considered a good conservation method. Lacing uses a sewing needle and strong thread to pull the work taut and to secure it on the back of the support board, using long zigzag stitches that run both horizontally and vertically.

Use an acid-free matboard or foam board for the backing board, and use cotton crochet thread for the lacing. For archival lacing, two layers of conservation matboard, or a conservation matboard on top of acid-free foam board, may be used. Lacing requires an inch or more of excess fabric on all four sides. To prepare a laced needlework for matting, use the pressure method for foam board or the sink method for matboard, described earlier in this chapter.

1. Cut a piece of board to size. Measure to determine the center of the board and needlework on all four sides. Position the needlework on the board and hold the four centers with T-pins pushed part way into the core of the board. Stretch the fabric taut while placing the pins, keeping the grain of the stitchery straight. Place the needlework face down and fold the excess material onto the back. Hold the fabric in place with several pins.

2. Thread the needle with cotton crochet thread—sturdy but not too thick. Do not cut the thread from the spool. Try to work with one continuous piece of thread, although this may be impractical on large pieces. A continuous thread helps to provide even tension. Starting in the upper left corner, fold the edge of the fabric under about ¼" (6 mm) or so, to make a strong support for the stitches. Insert the needle just above the folded edge, and begin to make long stitches that reach from one side of the work to the opposite side (which is also folded for support). Place stitches close together (about ½" [1.3 cm] apart) to keep an even tension on the needlework. When the thread in the needle is used, pull more thread from the spool and ease it through the previous lacing. Continue stitching from side to side.

This lacing is completed, and the last thread is ready to be tied. Two different colors of embroidery floss were used for the lacing so the photograph could show the two directions of stitches more clearly.

3. When the lacing reaches the opposite corner, tie off the thread where the needle last stitched. Gently pull the stitches taut as necessary, working back to the spool. Do not tie it yet—wait until the other two sides are laced, in case any adjustments must be made. Repeat the process in the opposite direction. Make any final adjustments and tie off all threads.

Sewing (Tacking)

This is not continuous, interlocking stitches, but instead refers to single stitches that could be called tacking. This method places the least possible stress on the work and provides sufficient support for framing antique needlework, such as vintage samplers, or any fragile piece that cannot endure the stress of taut stretching. This method is used for any needlework that will be "floated" in a frame and for needlework with an unusual shape, such as a crocheted doily. The backing board for this method should be cut to fit the frame size, whether or not the piece will be matted. Matboard (fabric-covered is preferred) is normally used for the backing board.

 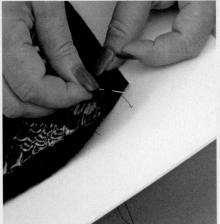 

1. Lay the needlework on the backing board to determine placement. With a pushpin or small awl, make pairs of holes for the needle about ¼" (6 mm) apart at strategic support points. Be careful not to pierce threads on the needlework. Each pair of holes will make one stitch.

2. Thread a sewing needle with thread in a color that matches the color of the needlework fabric. From the back of the board, bring the threaded needle up through one of the holes and through the needlework. Move the needle about ⅛" (3 mm) to ¼" (6 mm) and pass it down through the second hole of that pair.

3. Tie a knot in the two threads at the back of the board, and tape the knot to the back of the board for security. Repeat until all stitches are completed. Some framers make a series of stitches with one thread rather than tying off each stitch individually. Try both ways: Whichever seems to work best is fine.

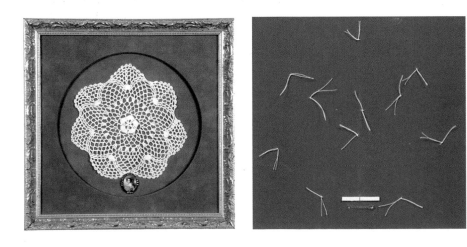

(far left) This crocheted doily is held in place with eleven individual stitches. It is framed along with an antique broach.

(left) The eleven individual stitches are visible on the back of the support board; a red board was used to make the stitches more visible in the photograph. The broach has a bar pin, which has been pressed through a slot in the support board, and it also has a loop at the top, so it could be worn on a chain. The loop is held with the slot and slide method, discussed in Shadow Boxes (page 162).

Sewing (Overall Support)

This is used to support a soft, large piece of fabric, such as a quilt block or a flag. It is done with tacking stitches as described opposite, but they are placed at many spots over the entire surface of the fabric. Use the fewest stitches possible to support the work without areas of slumping. As with the sewing (tacking) method, the backing board should be cut to fit the frame size.

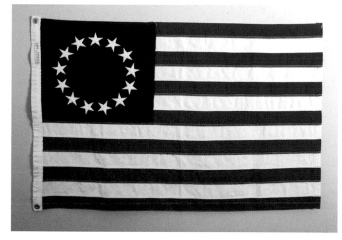

Choose the placement of stitches strategically, making the fewest stitches possible while providing overall support. A 12" (30.5 cm) quilt block may need only a dozen stitches. An antique flag like this one may require forty stitches, staggered throughout the body of the flag, with lots of support stitches at the top.

Taping

This is a quick DIY method but not a good method for valued needlework, because it does not provide a secure hold and it places adhesive in direct contact with the needlework. If there is plenty of excess fabric around the needlework design area, and the tape touches this excess, is that a problem? Conservation framing standards say yes; many DIY framers say no.

Use a good quality tape, such as Magic Mending Tape or a pH-neutral double-sided tape. For pieces that will be matted, needlework can be taped flat to the surface of a backing board. For unmatted pieces, wrap the needlework fabric around the backing board, and tape the excess to the back of the board. It isn't always easy to get a straight, square stretch of even-weave fabrics, such as counted cross-stitch fabric, so it will probably be necessary to lift the tape on one or two sides and realign.

Sticky Boards

These are sold in craft and hobby stores for mounting needlework. Some are sticky all over the surface of the board; others have a layer of batting that supports the needlework and a sticky back to hold the excess that is wrapped around the board. Choose a good quality, such as Perfect Mount, which uses an acid-free board and pH-neutral adhesive, to avoid possible future damage from acids. This is a practical DIY method but not an archival method, because it places adhesive in contact with the needlework. Follow the manufacturer's instructions for mounting the work, being careful to align the straight grain of the fabric with a straight edge of the board.

This sticky board comes with a layer of polyester batting on the surface and an adhesive-coated backing board.

Stapling

Needlework may be stretched with staples. For unmatted needlework, use a thick mounting board that can receive staples, a staple gun with stainless steel staples, and the mounting method for Stretching Art on Canvas (page 146). For matted needlework, staple the needlework flat to a matboard using an ordinary office stapler, placing staples as described in the pinning method (page 156) earlier in this chapter.

Spray Mounting

This is a poor choice for the health of the needlework. Spray adhesives discolor over time, which can discolor the needlework. Some of the adhesive is bound to soak into the needlework fabric and may not be removable.

Framing Needlepoint

Needlepoint is normally worked on a firm mesh called needlepoint canvas. The work is done with strands of yarn, traditionally made of wool, but today acrylic or cotton yarns, sometimes accented with specialty yarns, such as metallic gold, are also popular. The work is created with small diagonal stitches that cover the entire canvas.

Designing Framing for Needlepoint

Needlepoint is traditionally framed like art on canvas, with linen liners used instead of mats, and with no glazing. All of the stitched image is meant to show, except for what is hidden by the rabbet of the frame. Narrow, shallow frames will not be able to accommodate needlepoint stretched on stretcher bars, but otherwise any frame that complements the needlepoint is suitable.

Stretching a Needlepoint

After blocking, the needlepoint is now ready for stretching, typically on stretcher bars, just like art on canvas. The needlepoint can be stretched while still damp, or it can be left to dry on the blocking board and stretched later. If using the canvas stretching method, follow the steps for Stretching Art on Canvas (page 146).

Fitting Needlework

The process of finishing the framing (installing all of the materials in the frame, sealing it up, and adding hanging hardware) is called fitting. Needlework is fitted according to the way it has been handled: Is it matted? Glazed? Stretched on wooden bars like an oil painting? See Fitting (page 111) for step-by-step instructions.

This needlepoint has been framed with a linen-covered liner as an accent border.

Although a needlepoint is traditionally stretched on stretcher bars, it may also be stapled flat to a support board so that matting can be used. Notice the markings on the support board, which keep the work square during stretching.

Blocking a Needlepoint

Blocking stretches needlepoint into a uniform shape. Once stretched into position, the work is allowed to dry, setting the shape. Blocking also keeps the needlework from stretching or sagging after it has been framed.

There are some dangers to consider when blocking: non-permanent markers used on the canvas, bleeding yarns, shrinking or dulling of yarns, water spotting. Examine the needlework carefully and test an obscure area before blocking.

Steam Blocking a Needlepoint

The gentle moisture of steam blocking helps to avoid problems associated with bleeding yarn, sulphur dye, heavily-sized canvas, metallic thread, and cheap kits. This method is also very fast.

Materials:
- Blocking board
- Stapler or push pins
- Steam iron or steamer

1. Place the needlepoint face up on the blocking board. Pull at the top two corners of the needlepoint, and line up the top row of stitching with the lines on the blocking board. Push a pin at the corners to hold in place. Pin into the canvas—not the yarns. Do not force the pins deeply into the board—they will need to be removed soon.

2. Steam entire surface of the needlepoint with the iron. Do not touch the face of the needlepoint with the iron. Pressing is not a part of this process—steam alone is used to relax the yarn and canvas so they can be stretched to their maximum size and pulled square.

3. While the needlepoint is still warm from the steam, pull the lower left corner straight down to line up square on the blocking board. Secure with pins.

a) Steam again and pull the bottom into alignment. Pin.

b) Steam and line up the right side. Pin.

c) Steam the entire needlepoint once again.

Note: The needlepoint can be stretched while still damp, or can be left to dry on the blocking board and stretched later.

Extra tough needlepoint? Use more steam to relax the fibers. Pull and steam at the same time. Be sure the iron is clean.

SHADOW BOXES: FRAMING OBJECTS

Types of Objects

A wide variety of objects may be framed for display. Some are treasured parts of a collection, such as coins, seashells, or thimbles. Others are unique items, such as an autographed baseball or a movie script. Often the items commemorate an event such as a vacation, a graduation, or a wedding. Framers use many different materials and methods for handling objects, depending on the shape, weight, size, composition, and condition of each item.

In general, there are two reasons why an object may be unsuitable for framing: It may be too unstable, or it may be too heavy. The unstable items are typically organic, such as nonpreserved dried flowers, food items, animal items (except hide, horn, teeth, or bones), leaves, or crumbling antiques made of wood, metal, fabric, or clay. Unless the item can be preserved, it is likely to progressively deteriorate in the frame. The heavy items are diverse, and it is a matter of judgment whether or not they can be supported adequately in a frame, and whether the wall can support the weight of the frame.

Framing for objects has a few special considerations: deep frames, strong hangers, and deciding how to support the objects securely and attractively in the frame. However, as with any framing project, the first step is design.

A shadow box with no matting creates an attractive display case for the wall.

Designing Framing for Objects

The size of the thickest object determines the depth needed for the shadow box frame.

This layout gives each shell its own space but keeps them visually related to one another.

Measuring Objects

Correct measurement of the length and width of a dimensional object is important, but the depth (thickness) of the object is critical in choosing a frame that can contain the object. Remember to include the space needed for glazing and backing boards when choosing a frame that is deep enough.

The Layout

Sometimes objects in a shadow box frame have a natural order, such as chronologically by date or ranging in size from smallest to largest. More often, the best arrangement is found by trial and error and is partly a matter of opinion. Seek a balance in the placement of sizes and colors of objects. To make one object stand out in importance, place it in the center, or give it special treatment such as a separate mat opening or a small frame around it.

The spacing around objects determines the visual success of the design. For a single object, the goal is to find a balance between crowding the object with too little surrounding space and making it appear to float aimlessly in too much space. With multiple objects, the goal is to avoid crowding but make sure the objects relate to one another in the design. Try different arrangements of multiple objects until a suitable arrangement is found.

The other design choices for a shadow box are made as for any other framing: What colors dominate? What is the character of the objects? Where will the framing hang? When there is a group of objects, look for a unifying color or use something neutral that is compatible with the items.

Mats for Shadow Boxes

Shadow boxes are often designed without matting, but matting can be an attractive addition to shadow box design.

A shadow box with no matting creates an attractive display case for the wall.

A mat fitted in the face of the frame gives objects a more formal presentation.

Individual mat openings focus attention on each object and help organize the design.

Frames for Shadow Boxes

Shadow box frames usually have narrow faces and deep sides. Typical finishes are oak, cherry, black, white, and gold, with little ornamentation. A deep shadow box can be custom-made by building a plain, deep rectangle of furniture-quality wood from the local DIY store, and attaching any frame to its face (with glue and nails). The sides can be finished to match the face frame or can have a contrasting finish. Some shadow box frames (especially those with a finished interior) have a "back rabbet" to support the backing board. Some metal frames are deep enough for shadow boxes, but for large or heavy projects look for the type that has two hardware channels (one in the front of the frame, one in the back) for sufficient strength. Too much weight in an ordinary metal frame can cause the lower corners of the frame to separate.

This moulding profile shows a shadow box frame with a back rabbet to hold the backing board that contains the objects.

Glazing for Shadow Boxes

The majority of shadow box frames will need glazing to protect the objects. All types of clear glazing and museum glazing are suitable for shadow box frames. Non-glare glazing is not suitable, because the surface etching that provides the non-reflective finish causes dulling and blurring when viewed at a distance of more than two matboards.

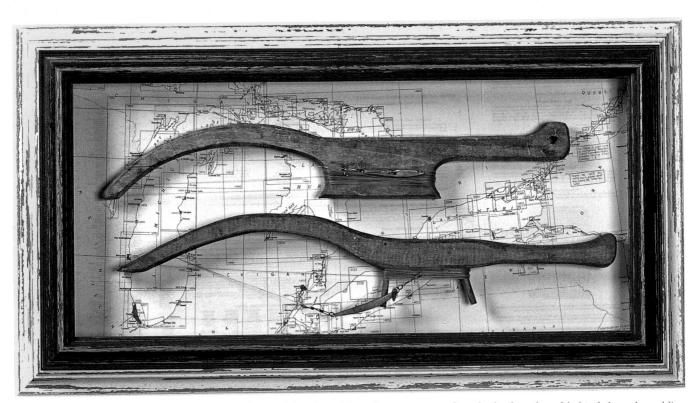

Glass protects these antique fishing poles from dust and handling. Note the map mounted to the backing board behind the poles, adding interest to the design.

Attachments for Objects

Installing objects safely, securely, and attractively in a frame is a constant challenge in picture framing. There are dozens of possibilities, but there are a few basic methods favored by professionals that are also practical for the DIY framer. Sometimes attachments are not visible or barely visible; other times they are more obvious. When attachments show, they should be selected to be as compatible with the objects as possible.

The primary rule: Be kind to anything of value, whether that value is monetary, historical, or sentimental. Attachments for valued objects should be reversible with no harm to the objects. All of the methods described here (except for gluing) are easily reversible.

Sewing

Individual stitches are used for clothing items such as a sports jersey, baptismal gown, or knitted baby booties. The goal is to make the fewest stitches possible while supporting the fabric. Lay the item on the backing board, arranged as desired, then choose strategic spots for the stitches. Use an awl or pushpin to make two holes in the backing board for each stitch, about ¼" (6 mm) apart. Use a sewing needle and cotton or polyester thread to make the stitches. Monofilament thread is suitable for some items, but it can break fibers on some fabric items and can stretch over time, making the fabric slump. Bring the threaded needle up through one of the holes, catch the fabric item with a small stitch, and pass the needle through the second hole of that pair. Tie a knot, taping it to the back of the backing board. Note: Some framers use a quilt baster with clear plastic tags (something like the price tag holders used in department stores) for attaching fabric items, but they are too visible in the framing for some people.

Most fabric items will need interior support to remain in position in the frame. This is usually a piece of matboard, cut to shape and inserted into the item before sewing. In sleeves or other areas that may appear too flat, crumpled tissue paper is sometimes used to give fullness.

This Victorian blouse has a matboard insert (cut to the shape of the garment with a craft knife), which will support the body of the garment. Holes made with a pushpin guide the needle and thread.

The blouse is held with stitches along the shoulders, at the center front, at the elbows, and at the wrists.

Stitches made with a needle and thread provide good support for clothing items.

This autographed jersey has a rectangular support board inside to create a flat shape with square shoulders.

Strapping

This is probably the most common method for attaching objects to a backing board, because it offers good support for many types of objects, from dolls to arrowheads. Each strap is like a large single sewing stitch: Poke two holes in the backing board at appropriate positions, bring the strap material up through one hole, wrap it around the object, pass the strap down through the second hole, and tie the two ends of the strap with a knot on the back of the backing board. Tape the knot to the board.

Thin materials, such as thread or cord are typical for strapping, but ribbons, strips of leather, strips of polyester film, and other materials may be used. Find something that is compatible with the object, and look for places on the object where a strap can provide substantial support.

Strapping would be the best method for attaching this boomerang to the backing board; several appropriate materials that could be used are shown.

Slots

For items such as military medals or broaches, the pin on the back of the item can be used to hold it in the frame. For a pin with a bar clasp, make a slot in the backing board, pass the clasp through the slot, and pass a strip of matboard between the bar of the clasp and the backing board to secure it; tape the board in place. For a pin with a point, poke the point through the backing board, and then attach the clasp to the point.

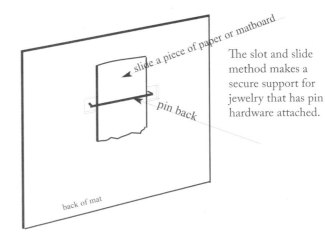

slide a piece of paper or matboard

pin back

back of mat

The slot and slide method makes a secure support for jewelry that has pin hardware attached.

Wrapping

Nylon tulle from the fabric store can be used to almost invisibly wrap some objects, especially baseballs, golf balls, and other items with a shape that fabric conforms to. Choose a fine mesh in a color that matches the object as closely as possible.

To use this method as part of a shadow box: Cut a piece of foam board the same size as the backing board. Determine the position of the round object on the boards, and cut matching support holes in both boards (backing board and foam center board). Adhere the boards to one another, and continue with the wrapping procedure.

This hockey puck is a good candidate for the wrapping method.

1. Cut a circular hole, smaller than the object, in a piece of foam center board. Wrap the fabric snugly around the object, and pull the excess through the hole to the back of the board.

2. Spread out the fabric, using a few strips of double-sided tape to hold it in place.

3. Reinforce the fabric with staples or glue to prevent slumping.

Suspension

This refers to hanging the object in the frame from various kinds of hooks and hangers. This attachment is not secure and the item can shift in the frame. It is not a good DIY method, except for some rare situations, such as for a sports jersey that will alternately be worn and displayed in a frame—the jersey can be hung on a clothes hanger suspended from a hook installed in the top of a frame with no glazing.

The blanket rests on a plant hanger mounted to the inside of the frame, while the sweater hangs on a padded satin clothes hanger on a knob attached to the backing board.

Sink Mat

A sink mat uses layers of foam board or matboard to create support for thick, flat items such as books, magazines, tiles, or puzzles. The process is described in Fitting (page 111).

This set of ceramic tiles is surrounded by foam center board to support the tiles and make a level surface for a mat.

A sink mat is not always deep. A single piece of matboard may create a sufficient sink for a jigsaw puzzle.

Mighty Mounts

These acrylic mounts are made to hold specific objects, with a little flexibility for different sizes. Coin, gun, spoon, and plate mounts are popular styles. They are available online from framing supply companies.

Mighty Mounts made for coins are an easy way to mount individual coins in a shadow box. All that is visible from the front are a few clear plastic tabs, as seen on the penny.

Hook and Loop

Adhesive-backed hook-and-loop material (such as Velcro) can be used for attaching lightweight, decorative objects. The hook and loop grips well, but the adhesive is not reliable over the years, especially on the material stuck to the object. Use staples to increase the hold of the portion of hook-and-loop material that is stuck to the backing board. Sew-on hook-and-loop material can be sewn to fabric items instead of using the adhesive-backed type. If the receiving part of the hook-and-loop material is well attached to the backing board (adhesive and staples), this method can hold heavier items such as a small rug.

Gluing

Gluing is easy and convenient, but it is generally not completely reversible, so it is not appropriate for valuable objects. Framers sometimes use clear silicone adhesive for strong, lasting attachment of stone and glass objects. Some also use it to mount coins, buttons, thimbles, and other small objects, although there is some risk of interaction between silicone and metals or calcium items such as seashells. Be sure to let the silicone cure completely (read the package for length of time) before sealing the objects in a frame. Objects can be removed from the framing by peeling the silicone from the items.

White craft glue is clean, clear when dry, and acid-free, but it's not completely removable. It is not strong enough to support heavy items. Avoid the temptation to use hot glue (the type that comes in cylinders for use in a hot glue gun) if you want the framing to remain intact for decades. It holds well for soft items such as fabric but not for metal, stones, and glass. It will hold at first, but over time the hold will break.

These stone-based fresco pieces were mounted to the fabric background board with clear silicone adhesive.

Multiple Attachment Methods

For shadow boxes that contain a variety of objects, several different attachment methods may be incorporated in one project. Consider each object individually and use an appropriate attachment.

Some shadow boxes require a variety of attachment methods. For wedding items, sew or strap hoops, garters, veils, and dried bouquet flowers; use small mats around photos and invitations. Glue paper items if there are duplicates and the framed ones are not needed for posterity; use corner pockets if they must be preserved.

Fitting Shadow Boxes

The process of finishing the framing (installing all of the materials in the frame, sealing it up, and adding hanging hardware) is called "fitting." For shadow boxes, this includes an additional step: making space in the frame between the glazing and the backing board. See Fitting Shadow Boxes (page 122) for step-by-step instructions and tips for fitting shadow boxes.

THE ART OF DISPLAYING
FRAMED ART AND OBJECTS

The Impact of Framed Art

Framed art is an integral part of room décor, and it can be used in every room of the home. Because it hangs upright at eye level, framed art draws a lot of attention, so it has a strong influence on the character of the room. Different settings have different needs, and there are many possible arrangements.

When arranging framed art on a wall, basic guidelines, current trends, and personal preferences all come into play.

Hanging Pictures on the Wall

Framed art for the home is most often hung on wall board, plaster walls, or wood paneling, but pictures can be hung on most any kind of surface: Stucco, cement block, brick, and even stone can hold framing if the right kind of hardware is properly installed in the wall. Check at a local hardware or home improvement store for items such as brick clips or masonry nails if hanging framing on materials other than drywall or plaster. If drilling is necessary, be sure to use the correct type of bit to make a neat hole without breaking more of the surface than necessary.

For hanging on typical walls, ordinary picture hooks are often the best bet. Very small frames, and frames with sawtooth hangers installed can be hung using a single nail with a head, but for most other frames, ordinary picture hooks are usually best. For frames that are wider than 24" (61 cm), two hooks are needed to distribute the weight of the framing.

Moulding hooks are designed to hang over rounded picture rail moulding installed on walls near the ceiling. Avoiding the need to make holes in the wall, moulding hooks are frequently used in historic homes, which sometimes have the appropriate type of crown moulding as part of their original construction. For most kinds of moulding hooks, a picture wire or decorative cord is attached to the screw-eyes or D-rings on the back of the framed picture; the cord hangs on the moulding hook. There are a number of styles available, from a simple "S" hook to embossed metal or fancy medallion styles.

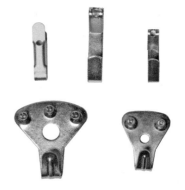

(above) These are common types of hooks for hanging frames on the wall.

(left) This style of moulding hook has a fabric medallion covering the hook at the top and a twisted satin cord that extends from the picture rail moulding to screw-eyes or D-rings on the framed picture. Here, the desired distance between the rail and the frame has been determined, and the cord has been attached to the D-rings. The moulding hook can now be hung on the picture rail moulding.

Choosing Locations

People hang pictures throughout their homes, and, fortunately, most locations are fine for most art; but there are some potential problems that should be considered when choosing where art will hang.

Light

Light is necessary to enjoy viewing framed art; unfortunately, light is potentially damaging to most types of art. It is always prudent to avoid hanging framed art in direct sunlight. UV-filtering glazing is very helpful, lessening the impact of light, but it is not a complete shield. All types of light (natural, incandescent, fluorescent, and so on) can be harmful to some degree. The amount of harm varies widely: Some photographs and posters hang in ordinary home lighting for a decade with no noticeable change, while a watercolor or ink-jet print may fade distinctly within a year. Unfortunately, the only way to know for certain that art is susceptible to fading is through observation—and the damage is not reversible. Protection from light is the best safeguard for valuable art.

Track lighting is a good way to feature an area of a room, but the direct beam can be too intense for light-sensitive art. Oil and acrylic paintings can usually tolerate a lot of light. For other types of art that will be lighted, use UV-filtering glazing and minimize the use of the light if the art is valuable.

Picture lights, which hang on the wall above an individual picture, are most often used with oil or acrylic paintings, but they may be used on other types of art as well. The classic style is a half-round cylinder that houses a long lightbulb, but some newer versions are small domes that use a halogen bulb. Picture lights are available in several finishes to suit room décor, such as black, chrome, and antique brass, but shiny brass is the most common. Most have a visible cord trailing down the wall, but the very long life for frequent use of these bulbs make them worthwhile. There are also battery-operated versions, which eliminate the cord and the need for an electrical outlet: Battery life is now up to seventy-two hours with LED bulbs—still not convenient for regular everyday use, but very reasonable for occasional use such as over a mantle.

These prints are never exposed to direct daylight. It will probably be many years before exposure to indirect daylight and incandescent light affects the colors of the art.

Moisture

Anywhere significant dampness is present—bathrooms, screened porches, beach houses—framed pictures may suffer from mold and mildew, and there may be buckling of paper art and mats or warping of wood frames. Full mounting helps keep the art stable but does not prevent mold. Some framers find that using some type of thin plastic sheet as a dust cover, along with glazing in the front of the frame, offers some protection from moisture damage. For decorative art, having art laminated before framing is another solution.

Temperature Changes

Extreme heat and extreme cold can cause problems for framed art, but most often it is extreme changes in temperature that do the damage. This is usually a moisture problem, because moisture can condense inside a picture frame during extreme temperature changes. Damage typically occurs in storage (cold garages or hot attics) rather than when hanging on the wall, but any room without controlled temperatures is suspect.

Smoke, Grease, and Other Airborne Particles

This is a problem for frames without glazing. If artwork is covered with glass or acrylic, airborne particles land on the surface of the glazing and can be removed by cleaning. Unglazed art should be protected from locations that risk excessive exposure, such as kitchens and fireplace areas.

Oil paintings are fairly durable, with good resistance to light, moisture, and temperature changes, but they can crack, buckle, or become moldy in extreme conditions.

How High?

Hanging frames too high on the wall is one of the most common mistakes made by beginners. For a picture in a hallway, foyer, dining room or other open wall space, think in terms of eye level, so the eye of the average viewer falls about one third of the way down from the top of the picture. This is typically about 60" (152.4 cm) from the floor. For a picture hanging over a sofa or chair, the frames should be hung just high enough to allow the head of an average-height seated person to avoid the frame. If hung higher, the frame floats in open space instead of relating to the sofa. Frames hanging over a chair or credenza should be hung with a similar guideline: close enough to relate to the piece of furniture.

The furniture, framed pictures, and accessories in this arrangement are grouped together so they relate to one another. Although there is plenty of wall space available to hang the pictures higher, too much distance creates a "visual tension" that makes elements of room décor seem disjointed.

Installing the Wall Hardware

The goal when installing wall hardware is to make the fewest holes possible in the wall. Planning and measuring are the keys to that goal. Small deviation from the plan usually makes no significant difference, but sometimes an error in judgment or marking makes for less-than-ideal placement of a frame, in which case there are two choices: Live with the error, or make more holes. Picture framers typically have lots of holes in their walls, and think nothing of adding another, but some people suffer a little for every new hole.

There are two important measurements when hanging a frame: the position of the frame on the wall, and the position of the hardware on the frame. For position on the wall, some Web sites and software programs about interior design allow the viewing of "virtual placement" of pictures in a simulated room. These can be useful for the grouping of many frames, but for one or two pictures there is no substitute for having someone hold the picture on the wall while you stand back and look at it. Some people make a template by laying the frame on a piece of newspaper or wrapping paper, tracing around it, cutting along the traced lines, and taping the template to the wall (with removable tape) to determine placement of the frame. Whether using a template or the frame itself, make a small, light pencil mark on the wall at the center top of the frame when satisfied with the placement. After the hooks or nails are in the wall, use a clean eraser to remove the pencil mark.

Frames with a Sawtooth Hanger. Many sawtooth hangers have a small raised dot that indicates the center. The frame can be held against the wall and moved gently up and down, allowing the dot to make a small scrape mark on the wall that indicates placement of the nail. As an alternative, measure the distance between the top of the frame and a notch in the teeth of the sawtooth hanger (this may be only about ½" [1.3 cm]). Using the center point marked on the wall, measure down and make a tiny dot at the determined distance. On the pencil dot, pound a nail with a head almost all the way into the wall—a bit of the head must protrude for the sawtooth notch to rest on. If the center notch does not provide a level frame, shift the frame to hang over one of the other notches.

A sawtooth hanger with a raised dot helps locate the center of the frame.

Frames with WallBuddies. One of the great things about WallBuddies is their ability to hang a picture level even if the nails in the wall are not exactly level. Measure the distance between the WallBuddies mounted to the left and right corners of the frame, and the distance from the top of the frame, and insert nails with heads at the two points. The multi-tooth construction allows you to shift the frame if necessary until the desired level is achieved.

Wall Buddies

Frames with a Pair of D-rings. Determine the distance from the top of the frame to the part of the hardware that will come in contact with the nail or hook. Determine the distance between the two pieces of hardware at that same point of contact. Using the center top mark on the wall as a starting point, measure and mark the placement of the two hooks; if using nails alone, insert the nails at the marks. If using hooks, place the hardware on the wall so the hook portion, not the nail hole, is matched with the marks on the wall.

Frames with Wire to Hang from One Hook. Find the center of the wire and pull it upward toward the top of the frame; measure the distance between this point and the top of the frame. Using the center point marked on the wall, measure down and make a tiny pencil dot where the hook should rest. Position the hook on the wall at that point.

The arrows indicate the distance between the top of the frame and the point where the hanger will make contact with the nail or hook in the wall.

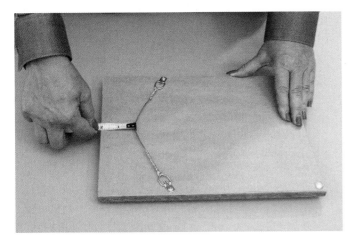

Lift the wire toward the top of the frame to determine where the center of the wire will make contact with the hook.

Frames with Wire to Hang from Two Hooks. Find the center of the frame. Find the approximate halfway point between the center of the wire and the sides of the frame, and pull the wire toward the top of the frame at these two points. Have someone measure the distance from the top of the frame to these points, and the distance between these two points. Along with a mark on the wall at the center top of the frame, this indicates the vertical and horizontal placement of the two hooks in the wall. If the alignment is not perfect, the frame can slide left and right on the wire until properly positioned.

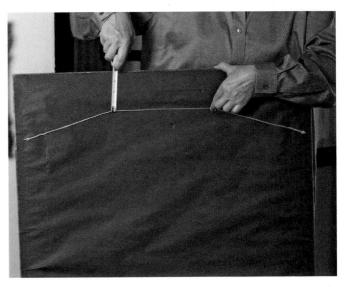

Pull the wire toward the top of the frame at two points approximately halfway between the center of the frame and the two sides.

Making Frames Hang Level

Picture framers find it difficult to tolerate picture frames hanging crooked on a wall. They are notorious for straightening pictures wherever they go—at parties, the doctor's office, a restaurant, a hotel lobby. When trying to hang pictures level, most people "eyeball" it; some use a level or other tool. Visually level is often preferable to true level, because this allows alignment of the frame with other nearby lines, such as a door frame or crown moulding, which may not be truly straight. Of course, even if it hangs level initially, daily vibrations and outright jostling eventually lead to a very un-level frame. There are two ways to battle this problem. The first solution is to use two hangers rather than just one: either two hooks in the wall, spaced apart from one another (for pictures with wire across the back), or two D-rings attached to the sides of the frame. The second solution is bumper pads, which attach to the bottom corners of the frame and stabilize it on the wall. The best bumper pads for "grip" are flat or rounded disks made of silicone rubber or polyurethane with adhesive backings. Most bumper pads fit on both wood and metal frames.

Look for the most logical reference point when hanging a picture. On this wall, the viewer's eye will seek alignment with the vertical stripes on the wallpaper.

Arranging Pictures on the Wall

Like most design decisions in framing, the best arrangement for framed art is a combination of conventional wisdom, current trends, and personal preference. The pictures in this section demonstrate some basic guidelines. Use them as a starting point for making decisions about placement and arrangement.

A Large, Single Frame

A large, single picture looks important and can visually "command" the wall where it hangs.

Multiple Frames of the Same Size

Pairs

Hanging pairs in a diagonal arrangement has been popular at times (such as during the middle of the twentieth century), but it is not usually favored.

Pairs of frames look best when hung symmetrically beside one another or vertically with one aligned above the other.

Trios

Trios of the same size frame are typically hung symmetrically, but this more playful arrangement is great for a fun look in a kid's room.

Sets of Four or More

Sets of four or more frames of the same size are usually arranged in a line or a block (square or rectangular) pattern.

Designing a Picture Wall:
Groupings of Mixed Sizes and Styles

A picture wall assembles a group of framed items of different sizes into a cohesive design. The frames may all be the same style, or they may be united by a theme (such as all black or all gold), but most often these groupings include a diverse collection of colors and styles. The artwork may be family photos, a collection of sports memorabilia, or a mixture of many different types of art. Other items, such as mirrors, small shelves, candle sconces, or other wall accessories may be included in the grouping.

There are no set rules for the best layout, but there are some guidelines. Try to create alignments, where the top or bottom of a frame lines up with its neighbor, but do not look for true symmetry. A grouping looks most natural when there is some "randomness" in the arrangement. Use separate frames of similar color to avoid making one area stand out from the others. Try to create a balance so no area looks heavy or skimpy.

Use minimal to moderate spacing between the frames, such as 2" (5.1 cm) to 4" (10.2 cm), to visually group them; if they are spread out too far, each one looks adrift in its own space. Also consider the "outer border" of the arrangement: When possible, it should form a roughly symmetrical shape (such as an oval or rectangle) so that if you drew the shape on the wall, the frames would look balanced within it.

This grouping is united by art theme (black and white photographs) and by frame color (black). Note how the alignment of frames (the bottom rails of the frames on the upper row create a horizontal line, and the top rails of the lower row create a horizontal line) provides a strong central symmetry that helps to "ground" the diverse shapes and sizes.

White mats and silver frames coordinate this grouping. The designer liked the "unexpected" low position of the frame on the right, but many people would prefer to see that frame raised to align with the top rail of the top center frame.

The frames are hung close to one another, leaving ample wall space at the left and right rather than filling the entire space available over the credenza. These three pictures form a roughly triangular shape on the wall, which creates a strong focus at the "point" of the triangle.

Rehearsing the Layout

To design the layout, some people are comfortable working on scrap paper or grid paper, drawing the frames on the paper in different arrangements. Most people need a more visual approach. If there are no more than six or seven frames, try arranging them on the floor, moving them around until satisfied with the layout.

If there are more than six or seven frames, it may be useful to work with templates: Assign each frame a number, then trace each frame on paper, number each paper, and cut out the paper frames. The templates can be arranged and rearranged on the floor until a good preliminary design is created, and then taped to the wall using removable tape (test first to make sure the wall finish will not be damaged by tape). Once the arrangement is finalized, the paper templates can be used to determine the placement of hooks for the wall, and then removed one by one and replaced with the actual frames.

Layouts for Numerous Frames

This grouping of pictures, which fills the wall with photographs, needlework, military medals, and other family items in a wide variety of framed sizes and styles, shows how a cohesive arrangement can be made from a diverse collection of pieces.

Layouts for Numerous Frames (continued)

Family photos are a favorite theme for a picture wall. Make an attractive arrangement of the first grouping, and then add new pictures at the edges over time.

"Off the Wall" Frames

There are ways to display frames without hanging them on a wall. Photo frames that stand on easel backs are the most popular example. Propping framed pieces on a mantel has a casual attitude that appeals to some designers, but be sure to secure the frames if vibrations in the room cause the pictures to slide. Floor easels are a great option. They range from simple designs (just three legs and a bar to hold the picture) to ornate styles with filigree. Wood tone, black, and brass are among the most popular finishes. Look for floor easels in furniture stores and home décor departments of other stores; a wide variety is also available online.

Photo frames of different sizes and styles can be grouped together for an attractive display on bookshelves, side tables, pianos, and other surfaces. This can work in any décor style, from traditional to modern.

Decorative floor easels made specifically for displaying framed art expand the possibilities for using art in room décor.

About the Author

Vivian Carli Kistler, MCPF, GCF, Adv. Vivian Kistler is a leading picture framing expert and in worldwide demand. She owned and operated a large retail gallery and frame shop for over twenty years. She has a degree in art and a certificate in finance. She also owned a craft store and a commercial framing company which supplied framing and art to hotels, coliseums, and hospitals. Vivian is the author of numerous books and videos, including the seven-volume *Library of Professional Picture Framing*. Her monthly articles appear in *Art World News, Picture Framing Magazine,* and *Profile* magazine. As an educator in the framing and art industry, Vivian travels the world training framers. She is certified as a Master Custom Picture Framer in the USA by the Professional Picture Framers Association and as a Guild Commended Framer, Advanced in the UK by the Fine Art Trade Guild. Vivian has appeared on several television programs including *Carol Duvall, Haven, Hometime, Your Home,* and *Aileen's.*

Acknowledgments

I would like to thank Sheri L. Galat, for her writing, research, and creative direction and Carli Miller for her artful scans and photographic detailing. Also, thanks to Carolyn Birchenall for her framing and demonstration skills, to Jim Cook and Roy Hermann for the use of their framed pieces, and to Barbara Schlueter, Heather Protz, and Andy Fiala for their photography.

My appreciation to the following companies for their contributions:

Equipment & Supplies
3M Company
Acme United Corp. (Westcott ruler)
Alfred Manufacturing Corp.
Alvin & Company, Inc.
Amaco
  (American Art Clay Co., Inc.)
Bienfang Framing Products
Chartpak, Inc.
Crescent Cardboard
  Company, LLC
DecoArt, Inc.
Elmer's Products, Inc.

Fletcher-Terry Company
Frametek, Inc.
Fredrix (Tara Materials, Inc.)
Lineco, Inc.
Logan Graphic Products, Inc.
Nielsen & Bainbridge, LLC
Novus, Inc.
Picture Perfect, Inc. (WallBuddies)
Pixie Press Paper
Ser (France)
United Manufacturer's Supply
Zig Markers
M & M Distributors, NJ

Frames
Eubank Frame, Inc.
Larson-Juhl US LLC
Nielsen & Bainbridge, LLC
North American Enclosures, Inc.
Omega Moulding Co. Inc
Abe Munn Picture Frames, Inc.
Roma Moulding, Inc.

Artwork
Classic Collections Fine Art, Ltd.
ColorSpan (Hewlett Packard
  Development Company, LP)

Artaissance™ (Larson-Juhl)
New York Graphic Society, Ltd.
Prudent Publishing Co., Inc.
Shorewood Fine Art
  Reproductions
U.S. Postal Service
Wild Apple Graphics, Ltd.
Loforti Fine Art
Roma Moulding, Inc.
Collection of Vivian Kistler

I'd like to thank the following artists whose work appears in this book:

Ansel Adams
Mary Lynn Blasutta
William Bougereau
Paul Brent
David Carter Brown
Dik Browne
Isabella de Borchgrave
Doriana
Luciano Duse

Roger Duvall
Joseph Eidenberger
Mario Fernandez
Wayne Finley
Barbara Fiser
Jean Fragonard
Sheri Galat
D. Giavvett
Judy Greek

Maeve Harris
Stanley Kareski
Clyde Kistler
N. Kitty
La Tarlatana
T. Leighton
Edmund Blair Leighton
J. Mark
David Marty

Alice Harris Marvin
Donata Menotti
Carli Kistler Miller
Vivian Miller
Claude Monet
Monlen
Danhui Nai
Georgia O'Keeffe
Sam Paonessa

Katie Pertliet
Nicola Rabbett
Henry Ashbury Rand
Richaw
Katie Saqui
John Singer Sargent
Deborah Schenck
Barbara Schlueter
Joan Schulze

Joseth Sham
Jim Sloan
Allayn Stevens
Marjorie Tomchuk
Vincent Van Gogh
Mort Walker
Cathy Welner, OWS

PhotoCredits

Page	Location	Photography Credits
	cover	New York Graphic Society Ltd.
4	left	Logan Graphic Products
	right	Columba Pub. Co. Inc.
6		Columba Pub. Co. Inc.
7	lower right	Classic Collections Fine Art, Ltd., Artist Roger Duvall
8		Columba Pub. Inc. art US Postal Service
9	top of page	Artaissance Inc. Artist David Marty
10	top of page	Columba Pub. Co. Inc artist Paul Brent
10	bottom right	Columba Pub. Co. Inc.
11		Columba Pub. Co. Inc, Artist T. Leighton
12	second from top	Prudent Publishing, Artist Henry Ashbury Rand
12	third from top	New York Graphic Society Ltd., Artist Jean Fragonard
13		Columba Pub. Co. Inc.
14		Columba Pub. Co. Inc.

Page	Location	Photography Credits
15		Columba Pub. Co. Inc.
16	top of page	Columba Pub. Co. Inc.
16	bottom	Abe Munn Picture Frames, Inc.
17		Columba Pub. Co. Inc.
		Columba Pub. Co. Inc.
19	center	Columba Pub. Co. Inc. Artist Isabella de Borchgrave from Wild Apple Graphics, Ltd.
19	bottom right	Columba Pub. Co. Inc., Nielsen & Bainbridge, LLC
20		Columba Pub. Co. Inc.
21	leftq	Columba Pub. Co. Inc.
21	top right	Columba Pub. Co. Inc Artist Monlen
21	bottom right	Omega Moulding Company, Artist Edward Raymes
22		Columba Pub. Co. Inc.

Index

Sources

This is just a small sampling of the numerous sources for the supplies referred to in this book. The products mentioned under each name are just a brief overview of what is offered, not a complete list. Inclusion in this list of sources does not imply endorsement.

INTERNET SOURCES

Framing For Yourself (Framing4Yourself.com)
Full range of DIY picture framing equipment and supplies; custom size wood and aluminum moulding; length moulding; fillet moulding; linen liner moulding; Logan framing equipment; Lineco products; matboards and foam board; Econospace™; Crescent Perfect Mount™ Boards; Mighty Mounts™.

William L. Day Company (framingsupplies.com)
Chop and length wood and aluminum moulding; canvas pliers and stretcher bars; matboards and foam board; easel backs; Lineco products; Logan framing equipment; Econospace™/Framespace™/Rabbetspace™; regular, nonglare, and UV glass by the box.

Graphik Dimensions, LTD (pictureframes.com)
Custom-cut mats in many colors; large selection of custom and ready made frames, including metal, float frames for canvas, linen liners and a few shadow box mouldings; miscellaneous framing equipment (point driver, etc.).

Frame Space (Artspacers.com)
Framespace™, Rabbetspace™, Econospace™, plus instructions for cutting and installing these products.

United Manufacturers Supply (unitedmfrs.com)
Professional framing supplier that sells to customers with a business name. Low minimum order. Complete range of framing supplies. Some items available only in bulk.

University Products (universityproducts.com)
Archival supplies for storing, preserving and framing art and collectibles; Lineco products; unbuffered museum boards; Crescent Perfect Mount™ Board.

Dick Blick Art Materials (dickblick.com)
Variety of wood and metal frames including some length moulding; wide selection of ready-made mats, including 8-ply rag gallery mats; sheets of glass and plastic in standard sizes; Lineco products; Crescent Perfect Mount boards; Logan equipment.

Frames by Mail (framesbymail.com)
Variety of frames, including flag frame, canvas floater and stained glass frames, bamboo, lots of metal colors, canvas-depth metal frames with front and back hardware channels for extra strength.

Art Supply Warehouse (aswexpress.com)
Matboards, pre-cut mats, ready-made frames, Lineco products, Logan framing tools and equipment.

Picture Perfect, Inc. (wallbuddies.com)
Sets of Wallbuddies™ for metal or wood frames can be purchased from this site.

Grignons Art (grignonsart.com)
Complete range of basic tools and equipment for picture framing, including matboards and chopped moulding.

GENERAL SOURCES:

Local Craft and Hobby Stores
Scout out local sources; there may be a lot available within reasonable driving distance. Many stores carry some of the products used in this book, such as Lineco products and archival photo album pages as well as white fabric glue, Magic™ Tape, double-sided tape, felt tip pigment pens, decorative papers, and a selection of ready-made mats and frames. Many also carry matboard and foam board, and basic framing equipment such as mat cutters. For framing objects and needlework, craft stores sell polyester batting, crochet thread, and embroidery floss, while fabric and sewing stores sell mesh fabric such as tulle, and stainless steel ballpoint pins.

Home Improvement Stores and Hardware Stores
Basic hand tools like hammers and screwdrivers, plus supplies like nails, screws, glazier's push points, D-rings, clear silicone adhesive, and measuring tools are among the many framing items available at these stores.

Art Supply Stores
Japanese paper, acrylic paints, artist brushes, matboard, mounting board, foam board, and basic mat cutters are among the framing supplies that can be found at art supply stores.

Home Décor Merchandise Catalogs
Many of these catalogs offer frames with mats and glass for customers to insert their own artwork. They often have white or off white mats in wood tone, black or white frames, but there are other variations as the companies strive to appeal to current trends.